IDEAS FOR TEXTILES FROM
THE CELTIC HERITAGE

Happy Stitching Drene

Barbara Howell

ideas for textiles from
the celtic heritage

Barbara Howell

contents

part 1

looking at celtic imagery

about this book

Celtic design is something that most people know about but here is a chance to look a bit further and to find ways to enjoy it through using it for contemporary work.

I have sought out a variety of styles of Celtic work and adapted the motifs for different kinds of contemporary textiles. Sometimes I have used the same design for more than one piece of work. I have used modern fabrics and a modern sewing machine to span the centuries.

I have tried to give comprehensive instructions so that readers who are new to embroidery and quiltmaking will be able to make a start. Some pieces are clearly more complicated than others! There are even some kits available to order.

I have also suggested ways in which the designs and techniques proposed for one project could be adapted and used in other ways. I find it very satisfying to work on a succession of related pieces – each one breaking new boundaries.

The gallery includes more of my own pieces that are not described in the projects section. There is also the work of some of my friends who have found inspiration in Celtic sources. I have included these because they are so different from my own work and I hope they will give more food for thought.

Once you are hooked you will want to see more. There are a great many books about Celtic design, some academic, some dealing with using designs for a particular style of work and some offering pages upon pages of designs that you can use. Some of these are listed in the bibliography. There is also the internet. Best of all, look for them in real life. I have photographed many Celtic crosses, especially in the regions of the British Isles where Celts were able to survive longer – some very ancient. I was delighted to find Celtic designs carved into the stones used to face the porch of a church in an old part of Rome.

The designs printed throughout the book and especially in the designs library can be enlarged in several ways. Scaling up with the help of squared paper helps you to understand the design as you copy it. You can use a photocopier to enlarge the designs and the magnification that is needed is given when needed for a particular project. Using a computer to scan and enlarge also has the advantage of being able to 'flip' the design so that it can be used on the reverse of the work and still point in the intended direction when seen from the right side.

Designing is a skill that I have had to work at and if I had had to wait until I felt confident, I might never have got started. I hope that some people will be able to use this book as a stepping stone; they say that 'nothing succeeds like success'. For other people, I hope that the huge variety of designs will encourage further exploration of this important civilisation.

history

The earliest civilisations recognised as Celtic date from 6000 BC in Central Europe but items in the British Isles dating around 1000 AD are also identified as Celtic. In my work, I have drawn on sources from Scandinavia and Northern Europe as well as the British Isles. I have found the styles differ according to the region of origin. Nevertheless we know that there must have been travel and trade which enabled new ideas to be shared. The monk who copied the Lindisfarne Gospels was Bishop Eadfrith. He illustrated his work in such a way that we are still fascinated 1,300 years later. He drew on sources from all over the known world for his decorative vocabulary and the chemistry that created the colours.

Celtic groups were sophisticated societies as can be seen from their many specialist artefacts, which must have been made by artist/craftsmen – blacksmiths, jewellers, stone-masons. They were also rich and well organised societies where expensive items such as torques made from gold were valued as status symbols. Ornate pins used to fasten clothing were often buried with their owners. Weaponry was not just purposeful but often highly decorated. There is evidence of recreation in objects used for games.

In the British Isles the introduction and acceptance of Christianity ran alongside the older Celtic religion. There are a great many items for use within the church that bear witness to the Celtic delight in decoration.

Interest in 'heritage' generally and development of leisure industries has led to the existence of centres such as 'Celtica' in Machynlleth and 'The House of Manannan' in the Isle of Man, where modern technology is used to help us to understand what life might have been like in Celtic civilisations.

Replica of early tenth century cross from Louth in Victoria and Albert Museum

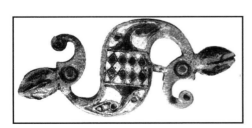

Dragonesque Brooch Circa AD100

SOURCES OF INSPIRATION

The designs used by the Celts are tremendously varied and whatever your design needs you will find something in this Celtic heritage. If you ask someone about Celtic design there is a good chance that they will tell you about the stone crosses that are to be found throughout the British Isles, many of them modern interpretations of the cross with a circle behind. Quilters are more likely to think of the intricate knot work used on such crosses.

In recent years, textile artists have written about using Celtic designs for a particular technique, and some of these books are listed in the bibliography. This book attempts to develop designs from Celtic artefacts for use in a variety of textile methods.

In 'Starting with Abstract Painting', Kenneth Jameson lists the features an artist may seek when designing as colour, tone, shape, form, pattern, texture, line, rhythm and harmony and balance.

COLOUR
The Celts knew how to find pigments to make colour and apply it to their ornamentation. The dragonesque brooch[1] circa 100AD uses strong turquoise alongside deep blue. Similarly the treasures found at Sutton Hoo[1] from the 6th or early 7th Century AD are strongly coloured and use other materials such as opaque red glass in metal harness ornaments. Again, brightly coloured bronze harness mounts from the 1st Century AD were found in the Polden Hills, Somerset[4].

We are fortunate that such materials have retained their colours over the centuries. There is a bonus in that the effects of time have also added extra colours on such items as the bronze Scabbard-Ornament[1] from iron-age Britain.

The early British Christian manuscripts, such as the Lindisfarne Gospels[2] and the Book of Kells[3] are a delight in their use of colour. Often, over the centuries, colours become muted and we assume that this faded effect was the intention. Being able to see these treasures helps us to understand how strong colours were valued and enjoyed by the Celts.

TONE
Many examples of Celtic Art have only the natural colour of the materials used. Tone is achieved by designs that are embossed, carved or engraved. Light and shade provides tonal variation.

SHAPE
The Gospel manuscripts are full of the most wonderful shapes, both large and small. Interesting shape can also be found in items such as the harness ornaments mentioned above and brooches such as the Tara Brooch[5]. Style was not restricted to important objects – look at the Decorative Head found on a Bronze-bound Wooden Bucket[1] as well as the overall shapes of vessels.

FORM
Many of the items that have been discovered in the various finds were made for practical use. Their shape is, to a large extent, prescribed by their purpose. Nevertheless a great deal of ingenuity has been used to ensure that

their form is also decorative. The Basse-Yutze Flagon[1] from 400 BC is ornamental in its shape as a vessel, but it is further enhanced by the form of a hound on the handle and a duck on the spout. The duck measures no more than an inch in any direction but is clearly recognisable.

PATTERN

Pattern seems to have been especially important. Many of the exciting shapes used in Celtic ornament are repeated to make patterns covering all kinds of surfaces. Even natural objects were converted to patterns, such as the hair on the Apollo coin[1] of the 2nd century BC. The carpet pages of the Lindisfarne Gospels[2] are supreme examples of pattern. The complexities of knotwork have challenged mathematicians for centuries and in fact are still challenging computer programmers today[8].

Urnes Lions

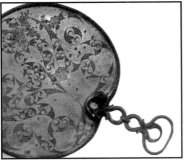

Desborough Mirror

TEXTURE

Perhaps it is because texture is so interesting to me that I consider it to be one of the most important aspects of Celtic Art. Many of the Celtic sources are 3-dimentional objects, embellished by texture. Sometimes there is a reason for the texture – maybe to strengthen a shield, or to create settings for jewels, but often texture is used for its own sake in decorative terms. An example of this is the Early Celtic Helmet[6] found in Amfreville-sous-les-Monts, France, dating from the late 4th century BC. Though made of bronze, it is decorated with raised patterns of gold, iron and enamel.

LINE

Lines are essential in two-dimensional objects like the Gospel pages. The carpet pages mentioned earlier often use lines to create pattern. Secular items, such as the late 1st Century BC Mirror from Desborough[1] are engraved with flowing lines and curves.

RHYTHM AND HARMONY

Celtic art uses careful composition of patterns, such as knotwork to fill a space, repeating motifs to create a rhythm. The animals depicted in the carvings on the Urnes Church Doorway[7] in Norway merge into knotwork made from their extended and elaborated body parts as can be seen in the lions in the Celtic Shadow Quilting designs and 'Celtic Hare' in the Gallery section.

BALANCE

Many people look to symmetry for balance but in Celtic decoration balance is often achieved without symmetry, sometimes by the use of additional knotwork. Many of the Celtic artefacts we see today were made for a useful purpose requiring good balance, such as the flagon mentioned above.

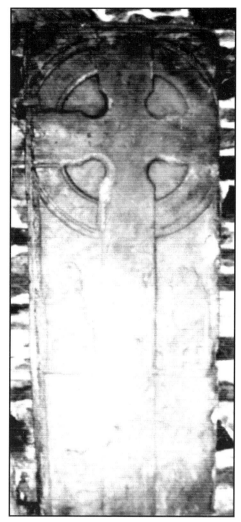

Manx Celtic Cross

Celtic Jewellery

[1] British Museum, London
[2] British Library, London
[3] Trinity College, Dublin
[4] Bibliography Zaczek
[5] National Museum of Ireland, Dublin
[6] Musée des Antiqu, France
[7] Replica – Victoria and Albert Museum, London
[8] Bibliography Sloss

part 2

projects

celtic shadow quilting technique

For colour photographs see pages 35/36
This is a technique that I have developed from traditional shadow quilting. Shadow quilting depends upon shapes cut from fabric placed on a background layer, showing through a layer of fine fabric such as chiffon. Stitching around the shapes holds them in place and makes the quilted effect. It can be worked by hand or machine. I have developed the technique to use modern fabrics and by the addition of an extra layer immediately under the sheer fabric. Many Celtic designs can be interpreted in this way. This chapter includes a library of designs that can be used for this style of work but there are others you may like elsewhere in the book. Sometimes you can make good use of more than one colour.

I always use motifs from Celtic sources and I think of my extra layer (teased out nylon fibre) as the mists of time. I started by using felt but I have moved on to fleece – the fabric warm jackets are made from; it is easy to manage and lovely to stitch through. The bulk without weight means that you do not need wadding to achieve a quilted effect.

CHOOSE YOUR MOTIF

There is a selection of possible motifs in this chapter. You will need to have the design enlarged. If the design is not symmetrical you will need to ask the photocopy operator to flip the design horizontally. I find that if the motif measures no more than 14 inches (35cm) in any direction the finished work can be used either for a cushion top or a small wall hanging.

YOU WILL NEED

Large piece of fleece for the background – say 20 inches (50cm) square
Smaller piece of fleece for the motif in a contrasting colour

Sheer fabric – 20 inches (50cm) square
Lining – 20 inches (50cm) square
Iron all the above before you start
Nylon fibre
Pattern for motif – enlarged to 500%
Sewing cotton of a colour to blend with the background.
Iron on interfacing stiff enough to trace through and large enough to cover the enlarged motif.
A waterproof marker

PREPARE THE MOTIF

Using a waterproof marker trace the motif onto the iron-on interfacing, drawing onto the side coated with adhesive. You may need to place white paper beneath or hold it against the window to do this. If the interfacing seems a bit flimsy, use a little masking tape to hold it onto your board while you trace. Before you iron to fix the two together, check the heat of the iron on a corner of both fabrics to make sure neither of them melts. Iron over the two layers, starting in the middle, fusing the interfacing to the motif fleece. Using your traced line as a guide, cut around the outer edge of the motif. There may be extra lines shown on the motif which need just a line of stitching – be careful not to cut these – indeed it is better to avoid tracing them in the first place. Keep the remnants of interfaced fleece as whole as possible to help you ensure the proper placement of the motif on the background. Some parts of the motifs are very thin – for example, the lions' legs.

MAKE THE QUILTING SANDWICH

Smooth out the lining fabric on a flat working surface.

Next place the large piece of fleece on top of the lining, right side up.

Arrange the motif centrally on top of the pile right side up.

Tease out the nylon fibre so that it is very thin and lay it over the motif and the background fleece.

Cover the whole pile with the sheer fabric, smoothing it from the centre.

Place pins through all the layers. Tack the layers together at intervals of approximately 2 inches (5cm). You might like to place additional tacking into areas where the motif consists of a thin strip.

QUILTING – CHOOSE WHETHER TO WORK BY HAND OR MACHINE

By hand – The quilting stitch is a 'running stitch' with equal sized stitches on the top and the back. Try to make your needle pierce the layers at right angles each time you go down and each time you come up. You can start with a small knot that you can hide by pulling it into the fabric. Fasten off each thread by working a few small stitches on top of each other into the lining. Choose a thread

to blend with the overall colour created by the background fleece when the sheer fabric has been placed over it. Do not be tempted to use too long a thread – 16 inches (40cm) at the most. If you have a choice of needle, use a 'betweens' as small as you can manage.

Place the row of stitches close up to the motif without stitching into it. Try not to allow the motif to move out of shape. The thickness of the fleece will help you and the raised effect will be quite noticeable when the work is complete. Remove the tacking and make up into a panel or a cushion.

By machine – I do not recommend 'free machining' for this work. The stitch to use is the ordinary sewing machine stitch – longer than you would use for dressmaking. Choose a thread to blend with the overall colour created by the background fleece when the sheer fabric has been placed over it. Use the same thread on the top and the bobbin. For machine quilting, I recommend that in addition to the tacking threads you place safety pins through all the layers in a pattern that gives you 2 inch (5cm) intervals. You can remove them as you work. If you have an 'evenfeed' or 'walking foot', you should use it. Alternatively, if you can loosen the pressure, then do so. This is to stop the pressure of the foot pushing the upper layers forwards, which would make the surface crumple. If you can press a button to make the machine go slowly, then do so – otherwise use your foot pedal very carefully. Place the row of stitches close up to the motif without stitching into it. Keep stopping the machine to lift the foot whilst you turn the work around the corners, leaving the needle down as you do so. The panel is small enough to turn easily under the arm of your machine. Machining is quite a lot quicker than stitching by hand – remind yourself of this and **take your time**. Start and finish by using a few of the smallest stitches possible and pull the ends through to the back of the work. Tie them and cut them close or thread them into the lining by hand. Remove any tacking and make up into a panel or a cushion.

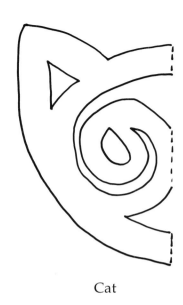

Cat

Dragon

Four knots

Goblin

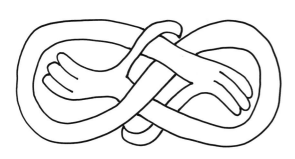

Linked Hands

Mask

Horns

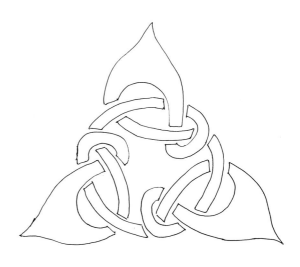

Triskele

st luke's carpet quilt

For colour photograph see page 36.

This simple patchwork design is taken from a 'carpet page' in St Luke's gospel in the Lindisfarne Gospels. The design of squares and half square triangles appears in a couple of options on the elaborate page, sometimes alone and sometimes grouped. The colours used on the gospel page are strongly contrasting – dark yellow, green, bright red and dark red.

The small quilt that I made measuring 54 inches (1.37m) square is shown in the colour photograph on page 36. The overall size depends on the size of the square unit and the number of blocks used. I have used four blocks and the square patches each measure 3.5 inches. This can be made smaller or larger and you may prefer to work in metric measurements. I have included for a 2 inch (5cm) border in the calculations.

TO MAKE THE PATCHWORK FOR A QUILT LIKE MINE

Make an accurate plastic or card template measuring 4 inch (10cm) square – the size of your 'patch' with quarter inch turnings allowed. If you want to work with a different size of turnings adjust the template size at this point and when making the template for the half square triangles.

For each block cut :

6 squares of colour A – burgundy

8 squares of colour B – yellow

10 squares of colour C – blue

18 squares of colour D – red

For the half square triangles, I like to stitch the diagonal line before it is cut – there is less

Diagram 1 showing the stitching and cutting lines for half-square triangles used in St Luke's Carpet Quilt. Thick line represents line drawn between triangles to cut along after stitching. Plain diagonal lines are stitching lines.

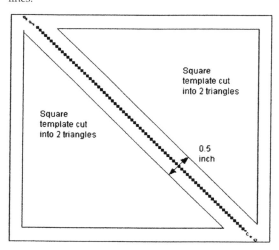

Square template cut into 2 triangles

Square template cut into 2 triangles

0.5 inch

chance of the finished square going out of shape. Make another template and cut it in half across the diagonal. Place the two halves an a piece of card and draw around them, as shown in diagram 1, ensuring that the space between the two triangles measures half an inch to allow for two quarter inch turnings.

Draw a line down the centre of this half-inch space – I shall refer to this line as the diagonal. Regard this new card as your template to cut around for the half square triangles. You need to cut 7 rectangles of fabric A and 7 rectangles of fabric B. This will be enough for 2 blocks because each pair of rectangles makes two squares. Take one of each colour and place them right sides together. Mark the diagonal line which you will cut along later. Your stitching lines should be a quarter inch on either side of this diagonal line. When you have stitched along both lines, cut between the lines and open up your triangles. Press open the seams, taking care not to stretch them. You can now use these newly made 'squares' for your block. Remember the order:-

Cut out the rectangles

Draw the diagonal line

Stitch the seams a quarter of an inch on each side of the line

Cut along the diagonal

Press seams open

Arrange the 49 squares of fabric on the table in the pattern that is shown in diagram 2 and stitch them together one row at a time, making 7 strips.

Then stitch the strips together. Work carefully taking accurate quarter inch seams and ensuring that the seams of the squares of one strip connect with the seams of the one you are joining it to. If they do not fit well, do not try to squash them in – measure to see what has gone wrong and open a seam to adjust the turnings accordingly. Press the seams open as you go.

Make 4 such blocks and arrange them on the table to ensure that the pattern is right before you stitch them together, once again taking care to line up the seams and press open the new seams. Measure the new large square. It should measure 49.5 inches (125cm) on each edge. Check on this – maybe you took slightly larger or smaller seams and when this is all added up you have lost or gained quarter of an inch or so. If this happens evenly it will not matter but try to ensure that the sides of the new large square all measure the same as each other. I will assume that you have taken the correct turnings in giving the measurements below. You can adjust yours if necessary.

Use fabric C for the border.

Cut two strips measuring 2.5 inches (6.5cm) by 49.5 inches (125cm)

Cut two strips measuring 2.5 inches (6.5cm) by 53.5 inches (136cm)

Stitch the shorter strips to opposite ends of the square of patchwork. Press the seams open. Use the longer strips for the remaining sides. Press the entire work carefully.

TO MAKE UP THE QUILT

Cut a piece of fabric for the reverse of the quilt. Make it slightly larger than the patchwork. Check that it is cut square and has not pulled itself into a diamond shape. Cut a piece of wadding the same size.

Diagram 2 showing arrangement of colours.

Yellow   Red

Blue   Burgundy

Iron the fabric for the reverse of the quilt and lay it out, right side down on a large flat surface – maybe the floor. Use pins or masking tape to secure the corners and the centres of each side to the flat surface. Lay the wadding on top of the fabric and smooth it out. Get someone to help you to lower the patchwork over the wadding – right side up.

Hand quilters. Start at the centre of the quilt and put in lots of pins through all the layers, working out to the edges. You will then be able to baste the work ready for quilting with the usual running stitch, ensuring that your needle passes vertically through the layers each time you make a stitch.

Machine quilters. Start at the centre of the quilt and put in lots of safety pins through all the layers, working out to the edges. I recommend safety pins instead of basting as they hold the work more firmly. Place them in a grid about 4 inches (10cm) apart so that there is nowhere for you to lay your hand on the work without touching a pin.

Quilt along the diagonal lines created by the half square triangles and echo this to make a series of squares on point as shown in diagram 3.

FINISHING THE EDGE
When the quilting is complete check that the corners are square.

Cut enough long strips of fabric 2 inches (5cm) wide to go all the way round the quilt.

I do not use bias strips when there are no curves to go around; the straight grain is easier to work with. Check that the length of strip is the length of the patchwork with the border plus half an inch. For the first stage fold the strip in half along its width and place the right side edge of the folded binding to the right side of the patchwork and stitch a quarter inch seam right along, leaving a quarter of an inch of patchwork unstitched at each end plus a spare quarter inch for you to mitre the corners. Repeat this process for each side. Stitch the mitres by hand and fold over the strips. Work by hand to hem the folded edge of the binding strips to the reverse of the quilt, covering the line of machine stitches. The edge will be strengthened by this neat narrow binding.

ADD A SLEEVE
If you intend to hang the quilt, stitch a hanging sleeve to one edge.

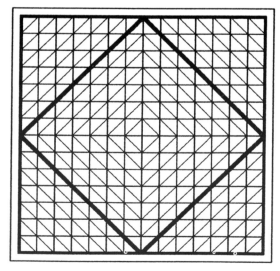

Diagram 3 showing quilting design.

SMILING OX
ON SIMPLE BAG

For colour photographs see pages 36.
This charming design was found in Dinorben, Denbighshire and is used here on an easy bag that you might like to make with children.

MATERIALS
Felt or fleece for body of bag measuring 10 inches (25cm) x14 inches (36cm). Denim is a possibility and any fraying would be stylish but it is not easy to stitch by hand.
5 inches (12.5 cm) square of fabric that will not fray such as knitted velour for motif.
5 inches (12.5 cm) x 6 inch (15cm) of 'Bondaweb'
2.5 inches (6.5cm) flowery braid for garland
8 inches (20cm) x14 inches (36cm) of lining
Embroidery thread such as stranded or perle
1 metre of cord for the strap

Be sure to do the tasks in the order given

DECORATE THE FRONT
Cut off a one inch (2.5cm) strip from the 'Bondaweb', leaving a 5 inch (12.5 cm) square. The motif is given here in the size you need on page 20. It has already been reversed so that you can trace it onto the 'Bondaweb' paper. Trace the ox head motif onto the 'Bondaweb' and iron it onto the reverse of the motif fabric according to the instructions on the 'Bondaweb' pack. Use the strip for the braid.

Do not remove the paper backing from the head yet. Peel off the paper from the braid and pin it in position on the right side of the head shape. Iron in place. Cut around the outside of the head shape.

Lay the head motif in the centre of the felt or fleece and iron in place. Stitch around the edge of the motif by hand or machine – I

attach cord ends at x, 6.5 inches (16.5cm) apart

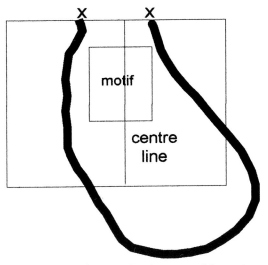

Diagram 1 . Showing the placement of the cord

used a blanket stitch. Embroider any remaining details, using the tracing as a guide.

ATTACH THE CORD
Stitch the ends of the cord securely to the felt or fleece as shown in diagram.

STITCH THE LINING TO THE OUTER
Place the top edges of the outer and the lining right sides together and machine, taking care not to entangle the cord but making sure it is machined through. Open up the work and

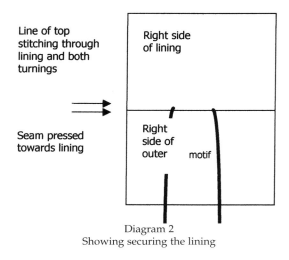

Line of top stitching through lining and both turnings

Seam pressed towards lining

Right side of lining

Right side of outer   motif

Diagram 2
Showing securing the lining

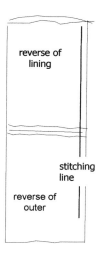

Diagram 3
Showing the main seam

reverse of lining

stitching line

reverse of outer

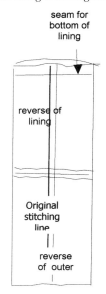

Diagram 4
Showing the lining seam

seam for bottom of lining

reverse of lining

Original stitching line

reverse of outer

top stitch near to the edge of the lining – see diagram 2.

MAKE UP THE BAG

Fold the work so that the long edges are right sides together and stitch down as shown in diagram 3, matching up the join between the outer and the lining and stopping short, as shown, because of the fringe.

Refold the tube so that the seam is in the centre and stitch along the bottom of the lining as shown in diagram 4.

Turn the felt or fleece over to show the right side, ensuring that the top stitched seam is just inside the bag. Ensure that the decoration is centrally placed and the seam is down the centre back. Press.

Draw a chalk mark one and a half inches (4cm) from the bottom of the felt or fleece and machine stitch a line that will form the bottom of the outer of the bag and the top of the fringe.

Cut the fringe allowing each strip to be less than quarter of an inch wide.

the
sun god

For colour photographs see pages 37.
The design for this panel is taken from a coin found in Denmark and is believed to depict Apollo. It is recognised as Celtic because the importance of the face is reduced and the emphasis placed on the representation of the hair in a kind of pattern.

My interpretation uses machine quilting with just one layer of lightweight wadding – there is no additional stuffing such as is used in trapunto work. However, you may prefer to quilt by hand and/or add texture by feeding in some soft yarn from the reverse when the quilting is complete.

MATERIALS

I used a 14 inch (35.5cm) square of :-
    Silk satin in a gold colour
    2 oz wadding
    Firm nylon lining
    A tiny bead to mark the eye

For thread I used semi-transparent machine embroidery thread in a creamy white colour on the bobbin as well as the top of the machine with a size 12 machine needle.

I used a blue water-erasable pen to trace the design onto the satin.

I worked with an embroidery hoop – I like the one with a plastic outer and a spring inner with a diameter of about 8 inches (20cm).

QUILTING BY MACHINE

Check with your instruction manual about preparing your machine for free machining. There are teeth set into the base plate that lies underneath the foot. These feed the fabric through the machine at an even stitch length. For free machining you do not want this to happen – you need to be able to decide where the next stitch is made so you need to disable the teeth. Some machines have a knob to 'drop' the feed, others a plate to cover it. Older machine manuals may describe this arrangement when giving instructions for darning. The foot to use may also be described as a darning foot but its purpose is to hold the fabric gently to prevent it lifting when the needle comes out of the work. Some machines do not have such a foot , in which case the tension of the work in the hoop is very important.

If free machining is new to you, this might not be the best design to start on so I am giving separate instructions for quilting by hand.

Before you start on the real piece test the method in as close a way as you can to the real thing. All machines are different and it is better not to be too anxious about it, so practise to gain confidence! Check that the tension is right – if it is too loose you will not obtain the texture you want. Your machine manual will probably have a diagram of how the machine stitch is made. The place where the spool thread wraps around the bobbin thread should be in the middle of the fabric layers. Set the top tension at 'normal' and work a test piece. If the stitch is not in the middle of the fabric you will need to adjust the tension. Try the top tension first but if that does not work, you may need to adjust the bobbin tension – there is usually a screw to turn but a few degrees turn will be enough.

You may like to keep your practice piece nearby so that if you are interrupted you can 'get your hand back in' before returning to the real piece of work. (I understand that that is what the hand quilters do to achieve consistent results.) Practise coping with the thread ends on your practice piece. Take one stitch and pull up the thread from below. Leave these ends where you can see them. When you take the work from under the machine you can use a needle with a large eye (crewel needle) to thread them through to the back of the work. There you can tie a neat knot before threading the ends into the wadding.

Use your blue pen to trace the design onto the right side of the satin. (I used a light box but you can use masking tape to stick the design and the satin to a window on a bright day.)

Make a quilt sandwich with the firm nylon at the bottom, then the wadding with the satin on top so that you can see the design. Tack across the work vertically and horizontally at 2 inch (5cm) intervals as well as around the edge. Place the work in the frame.

Start with the lines that seem to be easiest for you – maybe the straighter lines that represent a laurel wreath. Try to avoid breaks in the stitching. Some are inevitable and you need to leave ends of thread long enough to be able to take them through to the back. Stitch over the lines two or three times to make a strong mark and to camouflage the times when you need to take your thread around to where you need it to be. Move the frame as you need to in order to cover the whole piece.

When the stitching is complete, check that no thread ends are left showing on the right side of the work.

To remove the traced blue lines submerge the work in tepid water in the wash-hand basin in the bathroom (no soap or detergent, no squeezing or rubbing) until the blue has completely disappeared. Then lift it out to the drying rack over the bath and leave to dry overnight. You will find that the quilted effect will improve as the work is released from the frame and as it dries.

Stitch on the bead for the eye – move it around to find the best place.

Frame using a circular card mount – your picture framer will be able to cut one for you.

QUILTING BY HAND
This is a design that will lend itself to hand quilting.

HOOP – If you use a quilting hoop you may need extend your fabric to fit. This is a small piece of work and I would prefer to work without a hoop.

THREAD – Use ordinary sewing thread. Cut the thread rather than break it and use a length of 16 to 18 inches (40 to 45cm).

NEEDLES – A small 'betweens' needle as small as you can manage to thread!

THIMBLE – Your choice; there are several options of thimbles and finger guards and this is very personal.

PREPARATION – Transfer the design and make the quilt sandwich in the way described above. Instead of firm nylon for the lining choose a soft cotton.

STITCHING – Start in the middle and work outwards. Fasten the thread on and off by working two or three stitches into the lining. The stitch is what you may think of as a running stitch. Ideally each stitch passes through the fabric layers at right angles. Experienced hand quilters use a rocking motion to bend the fabric as they go, collecting three or four stitches on the needle before pulling the needle through. It is more important for the stitches to be even than to be small.

enlarge to fit 7″square

haversack with celtic motif

For colour photographs see pages 37.

This bag is quite easy to make – it does not have all the elaboration of some bought haversacks but it works out well for walkers. There is an easily accessible zipped pocket under the appliqué on the flap. Choose one of the motifs from the drawings in this chapter or another from elsewhere in the book and off you go. I have used the griffin, which some people think looks like a 'green man' and the circular creature that I refer to as a 'beastie'.

YOU WILL NEED

1.5m of 48 inch (122cm) wide firm fabric such as denim

12 inches (30 cm) x 12 inches (30 cm) of contrasting fabric for the motif – I used poplin

18 inches (45cm) x 12inches (30 cm) of lining fabric – I used the same poplin as for the motif

12 inches (30 cm) x 12inches (30 cm) iron on interfacing

2m of cord for drawstring

7 inch (18cm) zip to match the main fabric

0.25m of firm braid for buckle straps

Buckle to fit the braid with its prong removed

A paper copy of the appliqué motif enlarged from one of the drawings in this chapter so that it fits into a square measuring 8.5 inches (22cm).

MAKE THE PATTERN AND CUT OUT YOUR PIECES

Note: Half inch turnings have been included for seams wherever needed – if you wish to work with metric measurements allow 1.3cm

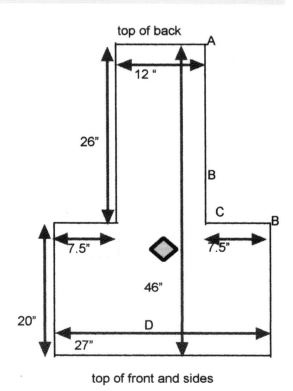

top of back

12 "

26"

A

B

C

B

7.5"

7.5"

20"

46"

27"

D

top of front and sides

Diagram 1

Draw out the pattern for the main part of the bag onto some plain paper. (Diagram 1)

The remainder of the pieces are simple shapes and can be drawn straight on to the fabric with tailor's chalk before cutting.

Use the pattern you have prepared to cut one piece for the main part of the bag.

Cut two straps measuring 27 inches (68.5cm) x 5 inches (12.5cm)

Cut two pieces for the flap – one in the main fabric and the other in lining, each measuring 18 inches (46cm) x 12 inches (30cm)

Cut one handle 9 inches (23cm) x 3 inches (8cm)

Cut a 5 inch (12.5cm) square of the main fabric then cut along the diagonal to make two triangles which are used for the anchor points for the straps. (Diagram 2)

Cut a piece of main fabric and a piece of appliqué fabric, each measuring 12 inches (30cm) x 12 inches (30cm) for the appliqué pocket on the flap.

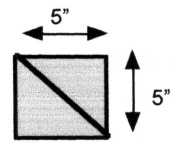

Diagram 2

WORK THE APPLIQUÉ MOTIF FOR THE FLAP

Iron the square of fabric intended for the motif and place it right side down on the table. Cover it with the square of main fabric, right side down. Lay the design over the two fabrics, right side up, and tack in place. Check that the motif fabric corresponds with the design. Machine stitch with small stitches through all these layers along the solid lines.

From the right side, cut away all the motif fabric that lies outside the motif. Neaten the raw edges by covering them with satin stitch or couched thread. The paper will tear away easily at this point. Decorate further on any remaining design lines of the motif.

ATTACH THE BUCKLE FASTENING

Cut 5 inches (12.5cm) of braid and stitch one end to the centre of the bottom of the appliquéd square so that the end will be enclosed in the turning. Neaten the other end well with additional stitching, as this will be threaded through the buckle on many occasions

Cut 4 inches (10cm) of braid and fold it into two around the bar of the buckle. Stitch both ends securely to the place marked with a diamond shape on the large section of the bag.

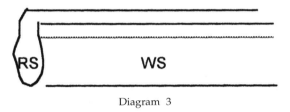

Diagram 3

MAKE THE STRAPS AND HANDLE

Fold the fabric for the handle in two along its length, right sides together, and stitch a half inch (1.3cm) seam (Diagram 3)

Turn it right side out and press so that the seam is in the centre of what will be the reverse side of the handle. Make the straps in the same way.

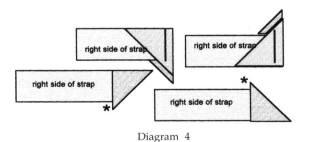

Diagram 4

ATTACH THE ANCHOR POINTS

Fold one triangle over the end of one strap, right sides together, stitch firmly as shown in the diagram and pull out the triangle fabric to cover the seam. Repeat, the other way around for the other to make a pair (Diagram 4)

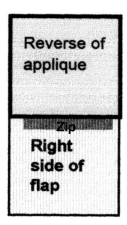

Diagram 5

INSERT THE ZIP
Stitch one side of the zip to the top of the appliqué panel, placing right sides together.

Measure 12 inches (13.5cm) from the bottom of the fabric you have cut for the flap and draw a line. Place the teeth of the zip on this line, right sides together, with the appliqué as shown in the diagram. Machine the second side of the zip in place. (Diagram 5)

LINE THE FLAP
Fold the pocket down into its position and tack in place. Check that the zip is working. Take the appliqué and the lining and place them right sides together. Stitch around two sides and the bottom, half an inch (1.3cm) from

the raw edges, stitching through the braid on the way. Trim the corners and turn through to the right side. Press. Top stitch if you wish. Tack the remaining raw edges together – they will be enclosed at the next stage.

STITCH THE FLAP TO THE BACK OF THE BAG
With the wrong sides together stitch the tacked edges of the flap to the top of the back of the bag.

ATTACH THE STRAPS AND HANDLE
Position both ends of the handle on the seam you have just made, with the handle loop on the flap side, as shown in the diagram. (Diagram 6a). Stitch firmly. Position the plain ends of the straps over the handle as shown in the diagram, (Diagram 6b), checking that the anchor points are pointing in the right direction to be sewn into the side seams. Stitch firmly.

ATTACH THE STRENGTHENING TRIM
The trim covers all the raw edges that you have just been dealing with. It goes across the full width of the back.

Open the work out flat and place the trim fabric right side down at the top of the back

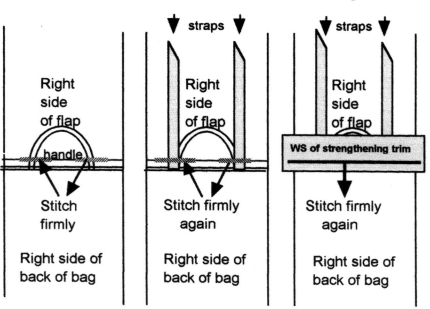

Diagram 6

of the bag, with the bulk of the fabric pointing towards the flap. (Diagram 6c) Stitch across. Check that all the previous stitching is under the turning. Fold over the fabric to expose the right side of the trim, turn under the raw edge and top – stitch in place. The raw edges at the ends of the trim will be dealt with later.

ATTACH THE ANCHOR POINTS TO THE BAG SIDES
Measure 12 inches (30.5cm) from the top of the trim down each side of the bag. Place the points of the straps marked * on the anchor point diagram (Diagram 4) here and stitch the anchor points to the back of the bag.

STITCH THE SIDES AND BASE OF THE BAG
Work on one side at a time and, starting at the point marked C on the pattern, fold the right angle, right sides together and tack along to point B. Turn the corner and tack up to point A. Ease where necessary and machine. Repeat for the other side. Neaten the edges on the inside of the bag, either with zig zag stitching or binding.

PULL CORD AND CASING
Work a buttonhole in the centre of the front of the bag (marked D on the pattern), 2 inches (5cm) down from the raw edge. Turn in a hem measuring one inch (2.5 cm), around the top of the bag. Thread the cord through the casing, using the buttonhole as the point of entry and exit. Fasten the ends securely into the seam.

Beastie

Griffin

"celts"
window
hanging

For colour photographs see pages 38.
This window hanging uses machine embroidery over two layers of semi-transparent fabric that is supported by water-soluble fabric. Scraps of lightweight fabric and threads are trapped between the two layers to add colour within the letters. A decorative edge surrounds each block and the blocks are joined together with unsupported stitching.

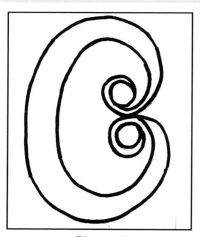

Diagram 1

YOU WILL NEED

A sewing machine on which you can work free machine embroidery

An embroidery hoop. I like the one with a plastic outer and a spring inner.

A water erasable pen – (you may think of it as a 'blue pen')

Machine embroidery threads, some variegated and some metallic and a good deal of white viscose embroidery thread for the edges of the squares.

Fabrics – the fabrics you choose may be different from mine but I used

5 nine inch (23cm) squares of each of the following:

> white cotton organza for the lower layer
> fine white tulle for the upper layer
> cold water-soluble fabric

Small pieces of fabric to use for the letters – chosen to a colour scheme

EMBROIDER THE LETTERS

Work each letter separately. Using the water erasable pen, trace the outline of the letter onto the centre of the organza square. See diagram 1.

Place the water-soluble fabric under the organza, ensuring that the chosen letter is the

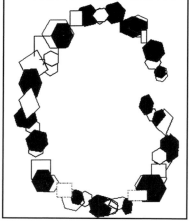

Diagram 2

right way round. Cut a piece of pale coloured sheer fabric to the shape of the letter and place it on top of the organza where you have marked. Add scraps of fabric, thread or fibre and place the tulle on top. Put in a few pins to keep it in place and tack. (See diagram 2)

Place the work in the embroidery frame so that the letter is in the centre. Remove any pins. Stitch around the outside of the letter to secure the layers and then embellish with machine embroidery.

MAKING THE HANGING
When all the letters are done, make a window template from a piece of card. Cut out a square measuring 6.5 inches (16.5cm). Place this 'frame' over each block and make sure that the letter is centrally placed in the opening. Using a water-erasable pen, draw around the inside of the template. This line will mark the transition from fabric to your own machine-made lace. (See diagram 3)

Stitch over the line in a fancy way, either free machining or you can use an automatic decorative stitch from your machine's vocabulary. It will mean changing from free machining to standard machining for this process. When the edges are secured in this decorative way, trim away the organza and the tulle from outside the square of embroidery, leaving only the water-soluble fabric.

Set out the letters to make the word CELTS in a vertical row (see diagram 4) and overlap the water-soluble fabric at the bottom of one letter with that at the top of the next. Line the letters up and make sure that the vertical distance between each pair is correct – I allowed 1.25 inches (3.2cm) between the horizontal rows of decorative stitching. Pin the water-soluble fabric together and machine over the existing decorative stitching to secure each pair of two letter blocks together. Reset your machine for freehand stitching ready to stitch into this area of water-soluble fabric to create your own lace. You might like to draw some guidelines on the water-soluble fabric. I worked a row of tall figure eights that overlap each other. I find it helpful to practise

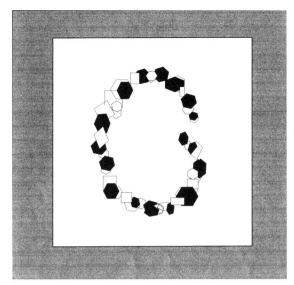

Diagram 3

the flow of the stitching with a pencil and paper. Practise stitching your pattern on some spare fabric framed up in the same way as your letters before you start on the real thing!

When you feel confident, place the work in the frame and stitch freely all over the space. Be generous with your stitching because, eventually, there will be no fabric to support it and you want it to be equivalent to the two thin layers of fabric and to resemble lace.

When all the letters are together you need to decorate the long edges. If there is not enough water-soluble fabric to secure the work in your frame you can stitch some scrap fabric to it, to extend it for the time being but be careful not to stitch into it.

COMPLETE THE HANGING
Dissolve the cold water soluble fabric. When all the stitching is done place the work in cold water and ensure that all the water-soluble fabric dissolves. It may take some time if you have stitched densely. Remove the work from the water and pin it out to shape on a folded towel to dry. Do not hurry this process.

Make a hanger for the hanging by stitching a rigid strip of white plastic along

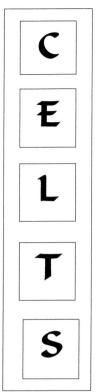

Diagram 4

the back of the top block at the top and making a buttonholed hanging loop in the centre.

Barbara Howell – Celtic Hare

Barbara Howell – Shield ornament

Barbara Howell – Mirror Patterns

*Barbara Howell –
Solomon's Knot Quilt*

*Beryl Jones – "My own design of Welsh
Quilting on a delectable mountain
pattern patchwork"*

*Barbara
Howell –
Dragon in
driftwood*

Project 1

Josephine Ratcliffe –
The Minster
Banner

Sheena Norquay – Our Pictish Past

Sheena Norquay – Pictish Puzzle

Josephine Ratcliffe –
Two Celtic Cushions

Barbara Howell –
Cushion with red lions
Project 1

Barbara Howell – Cushion with smiling Ox

Barbara Howell – Cushion with horns
Project 1

Susan Hinde – Celtic Cross

Barbara Howell – Stag Panel CSQ

Barbara Howell –
Dragon in Driftwood
Project 1

Barbara Howell – St Luke's Carpet
Project 2

Barbara Howell –
Simple Ox Bag
Project 3

Barbara Howell –
Sungod panel
Project 4

Barbara Howell –
Haversack with beastie
Project 5

Barbara Howell –
Haversack with griffin
Project 5

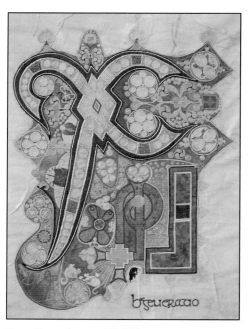

Jan Ransley – ChiRho

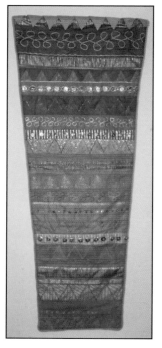

Barbara Howell –
Variations on a
theme from
Chepstow
Project 7

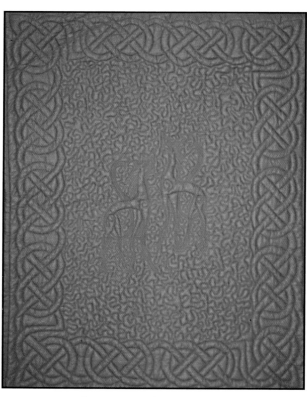

Barbara Howell – Blue Lions
Project 8

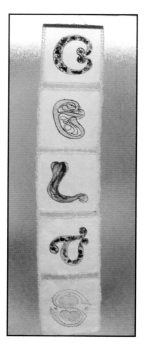

Barbara Howell –
Celts
Project 6

Barbara Howell – Waste Bin
Project 9

Barbara Howell –
Solomon's Knot Cushion
Project 10

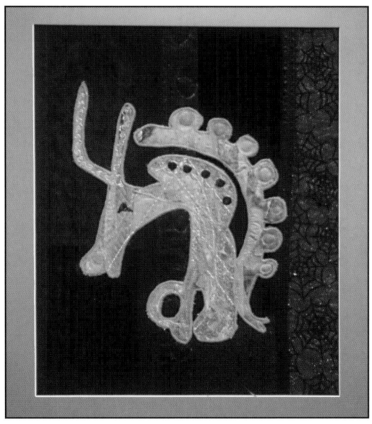

Barbara Howell – Stag from Capel Garmon
Project 11

Barbara Howell – Lindisfarne Corners
Project 12

Barbara Howell – OTT Cushion
Project 14

Barbara Howell – Celtic Fragments
Project 15

Barbara Howell – Quoniam
Project 16

'variations on a theme from chepstow' wall hanging

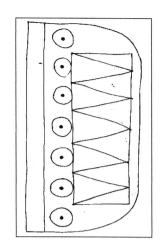

For colour photographs see pages 38.
The inspiration for this quilt is the decoration that comes from an enamelled harness mount found in Chepstow.

This wall hanging uses a limited colour scheme taken mainly from two striped fabrics which offered a good variety of shades and patterns. It is worked by machine and I have used some of the automatic patterns available on my sewing machine but there are many possibilities available to people who like to work by hand or have a simpler machine than mine.

The pattern consists of a line of circles and a line of equilateral triangles. The challenge I gave myself was to interpret these simple designs in as many embroidery and patchwork ways as possible. I worked each strip separately – longer than was needed to allow me to 'arrange' them for the final product. I added one more design, taken from another Welsh Celtic source – the Ox head from Dinorben – that I see as twisted figure 8s.

The photo of the finished work shows the variety of widths of strips and I am listing the methods used below but not the directions. Readers will want to improvise their own methods, depending on the resources available to them. Likewise, the size and shape of the finished piece is given here, but

only to help understand the scale of work. People whose choice of textile work is different from my own can set their own challenge.

My hanging measures 46 inches (1.17cm) long. It is 19 inches (48.26cm) wide at the top and 12 inches (30.5cm) wide at the bottom including the piping around the edge.

METHODS OF WORK USED (LISTED TOP TO BOTTOM)

Folded patchwork – 'prairie points' over striped print

Couched thread and borders

Patchwork triangles – alternate patches cut from a machine embroidered strip

Circles of recycled metal surrounded with 'cable stitch' in silver knitting yarn

Machine embroidery using silver and variegated thread

'Cable stitch' using variegated viscose knitting yarn

Metal circles attached with sequins and beads

Triangles separated by close zig zag filled with silver mesh and chopped up

threads, then covered with sheer fabric

Satin stitch circles with borders of machine stitched tucks and 'free cable.

Alternate triangles filled with free straight stitch and 'vermicelli' in silver thread.

Cable zig zag using hand dyed variegated thread.

Small washers coloured with nail varnish and secured with the help of sequins and beads, with borders of automatic stitches.

Triangles filled with free 'cable' stitching using hand dyed variegated thread.

Metal circles attached with buttons.

Triangles 'free cable' straight and zig zag stitching using hand dyed variegated thread.

Zig zag 'cable stitch' using variegated viscose thread and 3 row border worked in straight stitch.

Patchwork triangles cut from striped fabric covered with sheer fabric.

Free machining in silver thread.

Patchwork triangles cut from a strip of fabric embroidered with lines of 'free cable' stitching using hand dyed variegated thread.

MAKING UP

The simple quilting is 'in the ditch' and follows the horizontal joints.

The edges are finished with piping.

A sleeve is stitched to the top of the lining.

blue lions – wholecloth baby quilt

For colour photographs see page 38.
Wholecloth quilts depend on the texture created by the quilting and the designs chosen. This quilt uses the lions design from a Norwegian doorway set in a traditional knotwork border.

This quilt measures 32" (81.3cm) x 41" (104.1cm) and is made of blue glazed cotton. Providing that the proportions are retained the size could be increased or decreased and an alternative plain fabric could be used. Wholecloth quilts are normally associated with hand quilting and I think that this design would probably be better worked by hand. However, almost all my work is done by machine and so that is how I worked this quilt. Instructions for how to stitch the quilt by machine are given below but I have also included notes on how to work it by hand. The choice is yours.

The design consists of the lions motif (also used in the Celtic Shadow Quilting examples) which is set in a simple knot border devised according to the instructions given by Andy Sloss in 'How to Draw Celtic Knotwork'. These designs can be found in this chapter.

YOU WILL NEED –
2.25 m plain cotton 45 inches(115cm) wide. This is enough for the front, reverse and sleeve.
1.1 m 2 oz wadding -
Machine cotton a shade darker than the fabric or matching quilting thread
A water soluble pen
Safety pins

PREPARE THE DESIGN
Enlarge the border design here by photocopying. The outer edge of the border needs to measure 39 inches (99cm) at its longest point.

Enlarge the lions design on page 36 by photocopying. The design needs to measure 15 inches (38cm) at its longest point

PREPARE THE FABRIC
Cut two pieces of fabric measuring 34" (86 cm) x 43" (110cm) for the front and the reverse and one measuring 34" (86 cm) x 5" (13cm) for the sleeve if required. Iron the two large pieces carefully. Use the scraps to cut some strips of fabric measuring 1.5 inches (4cm) wide which you will use to bind the edges of the quilt. These need to be cut on the straight of the grain – **not** on a bias.

TRANSFER THE DESIGN
Use a light box, if you have one. If you have no light box available a window on a bright day will serve. Use a water soluble pen to trace off the border centrally onto the right side of the piece of fabric you have cut for the front, tracing onto the piece of the fabric that you have cut for the front, marking onto the

The knot work design

right side of the fabric. Then position the lions motif centrally within the border and trace this. The whole tracing must be complete before you start. Mark a rectangle an inch (2.5cm) outside the outer edge of the border. I do not recommend chalk because the work is handled a great deal when quilting and the chalk marks could be lost.

MAKE THE QUILT SANDWICH

Place the fabric for the reverse right side down on a flat surface and secure the corners to the surface – masking tape works well.

Cover the fabric with the wadding.

Place the fabric with the design on top with the blue design lines showing.

Start pinning at the centre and use lots of safety pins to pin all three layers together. Place the pins in a grid that leaves about 4 inches (10 cm) between pins. Some of the pins will be on lines you need to stitch but you can remove such pins as you go along.

Hand quilters – no need to use safety pins – straight pins first then secure tacking.

PREPARE TO QUILT BY HAND

This is quite a small quilt and it would be comfortable to stitch in a quilting hoop. The tension of the fabric in the hoop should be just firm enough for you to push the needle up and down through all the layers. Use a 'betweens' needle as small as you can manage to thread. You will also need a thimble and a finger guard. Cut the thread no longer than 18 inches (45cm) to save it becoming tangled.

PREPARE YOUR MACHINE

Put in a new needle – size 14 (90) is about right.

Wind two bobbins of the thread you have chosen.

Thread the reel onto top of your machine.

Ensure that your machine is positioned so that there is a good expanse of table to the left to support the work as you stitch.

WORK THE QUILTING

If you are an experienced machine quilter you may feel confident to work all the quilting freely. I prefer to work with an 'evenfeed' foot wherever possible.

The border has a great many places where you have to stop and start the stitching. There are two ways of dealing with this: -

1. At the beginning and end of every section make two or three stitches forwards and backwards on top of each other. When

The 'lions' design

practice the size of the squiggles with pencil on a scrap of paper. Keep this by you to refer to when you start to free-machine quilt.

The order of work for hand quilting will differ in that although the lions are the first motif the border will be the last. To start, tie a small knot on the end of the thread and bring the needle up though all the layers. Pull the thread though and, with an extra tug, pop the knot through the bottom layer of fabric. Work one small backstitch to secure. To fasten off the thread when it has been almost used up, the process is reversed. Tie a knot close to the work and take a small back stitch, bringing the needle out of the quilt an inch (2.5cm) or so away, popping the knot into the wadding. Pull the thread tight as you cut it close to the fabric and the end will slip back into the work.

BIND THE EDGES

Tackle each of the four sides separately, leaving at least an inch (2.5cm) of fabric at each end of each side. The rectangle you drew an inch (2.5cm) outside the outer edge of the border is there as a guide for you to stitch this binding. Place the edge of the strips of fabric along this line. Place right sides together with a quarter inch (0.6cm) turning, allowing the bulk of the strip to lie towards the centre of the quilt.

Machine each side separately then trim back the work to leave half an inch (1.25cm)

the quilting is finished the thread ends can be safely cut off.

2. You can start and finish by bringing the bobbin thread to the top. These threads can then be tied off later and the knots threaded through to be lost in the wadding

Stitch the lions first, folding over the work to allow it to pass under the arm of the machine as you turn it. Some parts of this design are difficult to work with the foot on. Leave them till the last and finish off with a little free machine quilting. When you have worked the two lions in straight stitch make another line of stitching around the outside of the motif – about an eighth of an inch (0.3 cm) away – no need to do the inside details.

Now move on to the border and work the knot design.

Finally work some free machine vermicelli between the lions and the border. Beware of working this too closely or the work will shrink unevenly. Aim to have a density similar to the border stitching. I find it helps to

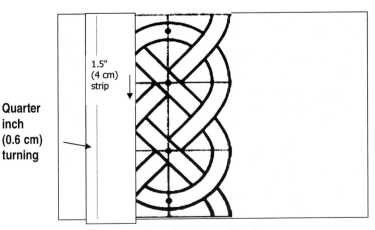

Quarter inch (0.6 cm) turning

1.5" (4 cm) strip

Diagram to show first stage of binding

of quilt beyond the stitching line. Turn over the binding and slip stitch in place by hand. Use the extra fabric to mitre the corners by hand, as you go, cutting away the excess after you have allowed for the turning and the 45° mitre.

ADD THE HANGING SLEEVE IF REQUIRED

Stitch hems on the short ends of the fabric reserved for the sleeve and stitch the sleeve in place at the top of the quilt.

felt covered waste bin

For colour photographs see page 39.
The inspiration for the decoration of this bin came from a spearhead, part of which was rusted away but which still showed some of the original engraved design.

The bin sides are made of card and the base is a block of wood; all are covered with felt. There are two embroidery techniques used, both using water soluble fabric. Decorating the top involved 'distressing' the edge of the felt and then stitching into it. To decorate the bottom of the walls of the bin – a fabric was created from fragments of fabric and thread, then cut to shape and appliquéd.

Size :-10 inches (25.4cm) high and 6 inches (15.24cm) square base

MATERIALS FOR CONSTRUCTING THE BIN

Firm card or mounting board cut as follows:
    4 of 6" x 8" (15.24cm x 20.3cm) for the bin sides
    1 of 6" x 6" (15.24cm x 15.24cm) for the lining the base
Felt pieces cut as follows:
    1 of 10" x 25.25" (25.4cm x 64.14cm) for the outer layer
    1 of 9" x 25.25" (22.9cm x 64.14cm) for the lining
    2 of 7" x 7" (17.8cm x 17.8cm)
    1 of 8" x 8 " (20.3cm x 20.3cm)
    (these measurements allow for half inch (1.27cm) turnings on all seams)
Block of wood 0.75" (2cm) thick and 6 inches (15.24cm) square for the base

DECORATING THE FELT FOR THE TOP OF THE BIN

MATERIALS FOR THE EMBROIDERY :-
    Machine sewing thread to match the felt.
    Water-soluble fabric 25 inches (65cm) by 4 inches (10cm).
    Small beads.
    An embroidery hoop – preferably the type that has a plastic outer circle and a spring to fit inside. This style of hoop slides under the foot of the machine without catching the point of the needle and can be moved along the work without removing the work from the machine.

METHOD :-
Place the long edge of the largest piece of felt (the outer layer) on a chopping board and using scissors or a different blade, scrape at the inch (2.5cm) of fabric along the edge of the felt until it looks as if it has rotted away. Aim to have some holes as well as frayed edges.
    Tack the water-soluble fabric under the distressed edge, leaving as much as possible free of the felt. Set up your machine for free machining, threaded with the same colour of thread on the bobbin as on the spool. Place the work in the hoop and stitch rough circles

measuring between a quarter of an inch and a centimetre. Stitch around each circle several times and place some on the good felt, some on the distressed felt and some on the water-soluble fabric. Aim to make the edge uneven and interesting. It is to represent the rotted metal of the spear blade.

Dissolve the soluble fabric to leave just the felt and the stitching. Pin the resulting fabric out on a folded towel and allow it to dry naturally.

Leave this on one side while you decorate the bottom section of the sides.

CREATING THE FABRIC TO DECORATE THE SIDES

A diagram of the shape is given here. You will need to create a piece of fabric measuring about 9 inches (23cm) square in order to be able to cut out the shape.

MATERIALS FOR EMBROIDERY:-
Two pieces of water soluble fabric about 12 inches (30.5cm) square

Many small scraps of a good variety of lightweight fabrics and thread ends in a range of compatible colours. The largest should not be bigger than small fingernails. Include some pieces with a metallic look.

Machine sewing cotton.

Metallic knitting or crochet thread for couching.

An embroidery hoop as above.

METHOD:-
Lay one of the pieces of water soluble fabric on the table and cover the central part (about 9" square) with your fabric and thread scraps. Try not to leave any gaps. It is quite alright for the scraps to overlap.

Cover the scraps with the other piece of water soluble fabric to make a sandwich and tack around the edges with some extra lines across the work.

Set up your machine for free machining and stitch in a random fashion all over the scraps. I used a thread the same colour as the felt.

When every scrap is stitched down, dissolve the fabric to leave just the stitched

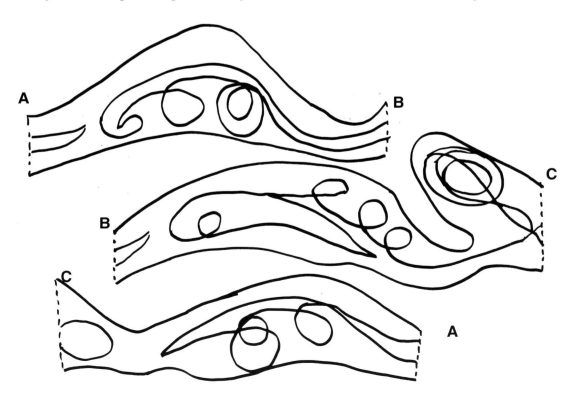

together scraps. Pin the resulting fabric out on a folded towel and allow it to dry naturally.

Enlarge the diagram on page 48 by 200% so that the total length measures 24 inches.

Cut out the shape of the ornament. You will need to join the fabric to make it long enough. Make the joints at the points where the band is narrower.

Stitch the shape to the bottom of the outer layer of the felt bin sides, using the same thread but with the machine set for normal zig zag sewing.

Couch the metallic thread to the outer edge of the motif and add some lines and loop shapes to the body of the motif as shown on the diagram.

MAKING UP THE SIDES

Stitch some beads randomly in small groups amongst the circles that are worked on the felt at the top of the work.

Hand stitch the top of the lining to the inside of the embroidered felt, matching up the long bottom edges and allowing the circles to stand above the lining. Stitch on some more beads around the top along the joint where the lining is stitched on to the embroidered outer so that they can be seen from the inside of the bin.

Place the four pieces of card, side by side, between the lining and the outer layer. Using thread to match the felt, work a single line of running stitch between the long sides of the cards, close to the card at each end and along the bottom. Hand-stitch the work into a square tube.

MAKING UP THE BIN

Use the two 7 inch (17.8cm) squares to cover the 6 inch (15.24cm) square of card. Hand stitch around the edges.

Hand stitch this to the base of the square tube you have made.

Place the block of wood in the centre of the 8" square felt and stitch to cover the base and sides, clipping away the felt where you need to.

Use PVA glue to attach the bin to it base.

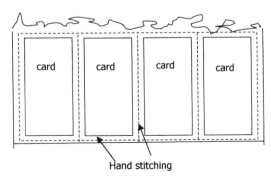

Diagram to show card stitched in place prior to stitching ends together to make a tube.

solomon's knot cushion

For colour photographs see page 39.
Knots are a popular theme in Celtic art. This square knot is known as King Solomon's Knot and is translated here into a square patchwork block.

The size of the block given here is 12 inches (30.5cm) to form the centre of a 16 inch (40.64cm) square cushion. A number of such blocks, joined together can be used to make a quilt, with or without sashing strips.

MATERIALS.

FOR THE PATCHWORK BLOCK -
Choose a striped fabric that has straight stripes, but one where there is a variety of stripes – not a "candy stripe". Look in the furnishing section if you cannot find a fabric intended for patchwork. A metre of fabric should be enough, provided that the stripes are repeated in the right variety. You will need 18 inches (45.72 cm) of 3 inch (7.62cm) wide striped fabric and 72 inches (2m) of 3.75 (9.52 cm) wide fabric. The wider fabric needs to be the same as the 3 inch (7.62cm) one but with an extra stripe to make the four house shapes (these are red in my cushion – see page 39).

You will also need to find a fairly plain section of the fabric from which to cut the centre square (B in diagram a) and the four small triangles (C in diagram a).

FOR THE BORDER -
You can use some more of the striped fabric but a toning plain works well. You will need 4 pieces measuring 16.5 inches (41.91cm) by 2.5 inches (6.35cm).

TEMPLATES

The shapes shown in diagram a are the exact size of the finished patches so that you can trace them. If you choose to photocopy the shapes make sure that there is no distortion. Use template plastic or card to prepare the templates and work accurately.

Mark them with
• their letters
• the number to cut
• the edge that must always have the same stripe on it as shown on the diagram, to help you make the stripes work together – one long edge of A and E and the second to the shortest edge of D
• the 'notches' to help you line up the patches prior to stitching

CUTTING OUT

For the patchwork

Check that the pattern of stripes follows the directional lines shown on the templates and that the additional stripe is at the narrow end of templates D and E. Place the templates so that the line of the quarter inch turning for template A and the lines marked on templates D and E fall on the division between the same two stripes of your fabric.

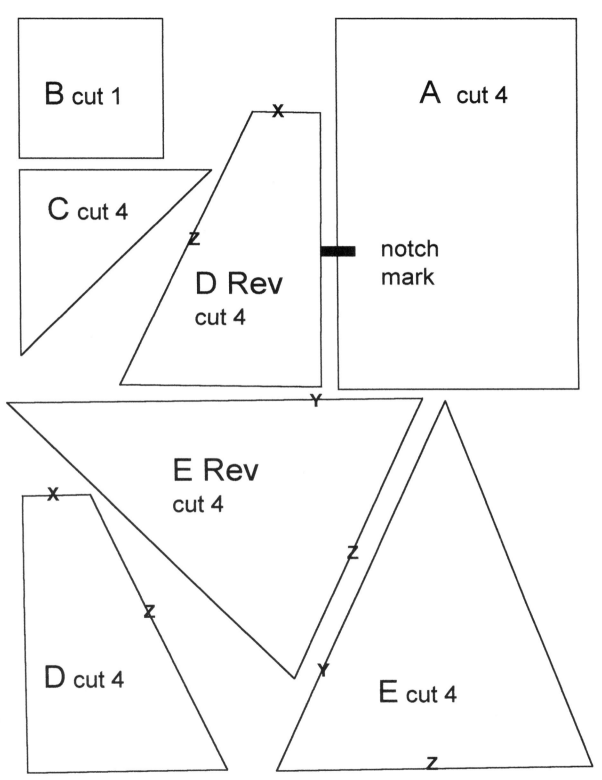

B cut 1

A cut 4

C cut 4

X

z

D Rev
cut 4

notch
mark

Y

E Rev
cut 4

X

z

Y

z

D cut 4

E cut 4

z

Diagram a – templates for patchwork

FOR THE BORDER

If you are using more stripes, decide which colour is to go on the outside. Place all 4 strips so that this colour is in the same position in the pile and cut off a half square triangle from each end. – See diagram j.

Remember to add turnings when cutting out the fabric.

SEAM ALLOWANCE.

I recommend a quarter inch throughout but you may prefer a metric measurement. Take great care with this or else the geometry will not work.

BEFORE YOU START TO SEW

Lay out your pieces to check that the stripes run in the way that you intended. The pieces will not fit very well because of the turnings but it is reassuring to see how the pattern forms. The patchwork consists of a pieced central square, set on point, with a small corner stitched to each side – this makes a strip with pointed ends. A 'large corner' is then stitched to each side of the strip. I think of the small corner section – consisting of 2 of each of D and E – as a 'house shape'.

PIECE THE SQUARE CENTRE OF THE BLOCK.

This central square is a variation of log cabin that allows all the logs to be of equal length. Follow the steps in diagrams b to e to see how.

Take a strip of A and the square B and place right sides together with the square over the left hand side of A and one side of the square reaching from the corner to the notch on the edge of A. Start stitching at the end and sew to the notch – diagram b. Open the work out and press both turnings towards A as in diagram c.

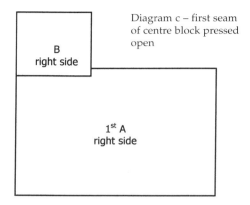

Diagram c – first seam of centre block pressed open

B right side

1st A right side

Use a second A strip to join to the end of the first and the square, as shown in diagram d, again stitching the notched edge, then opening the work and pressing the seam towards the outside as in diagram e.

Stitch on the remaining two A patches in the same way.

Complete the first seam as the final log slots into place to make the square centre block as shown in diagram f.

notch

Diagram b – first seam of centre block

1st Seam

reverse side B

Seam line for final seam of centre block

1st A right side

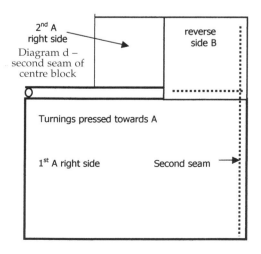

2nd A right side

Diagram d – second seam of centre block

reverse side B

Turnings pressed towards A

1st A right side

Second seam

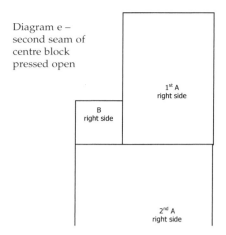

Diagram e –
second seam of
centre block
pressed open

1st A
right side

B
right side

2nd A
right side

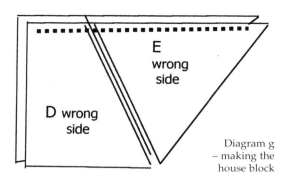

E
wrong
side

D wrong
side

Diagram g
– making the
house block

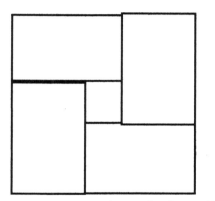

Diagram f – completed centre block

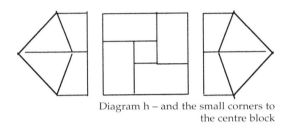

Diagram h – and the small corners to
the centre block

PIECE THE TWO LARGE CORNERS.

Start by piecing two house blocks like the
smaller corners and add a triangle C to each
side to make two large pieced triangles. Press
open the seams. – See diagram i.

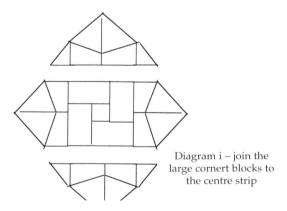

Diagram i – join the
large cornert blocks to
the centre strip

PIECE THE TWO SMALL CORNERS.

For each small corner ('house block') you will
need 1 piece E and an E reverse, 1 piece D
and a D reverse. Take care to match up the
stripes and seam E to D and reverse E to
reverse D as in diagram g. This time, press
open the seams before joining the two pairs
together.

JOIN THE SMALL CORNERS TO THE
CENTRE OF THE BLOCK.

Join these two house shapes to the centre of
the block to make a strip with pointed ends –
see diagram h. Press open the seams.

JOIN THE LARGE CORNERS TO THE
CENTRE STRIP OF THE BLOCK.

Stitch the long sides of these triangles to the
sides of the strip – see diagram i. Press open
the seams.

ADD THE MITRED BORDER.
Stitch the shorter side of each strip to a side
of the block and join up the angles to make
the mitres.

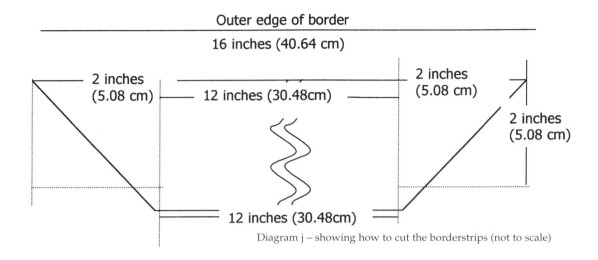

Outer edge of border

16 inches (40.64 cm)

2 inches
(5.08 cm)

12 inches (30.48cm)

2 inches
(5.08 cm)

2 inches
(5.08 cm)

12 inches (30.48cm)

Diagram j – showing how to cut the borderstrips (not to scale)

the stag from capel garmon panel

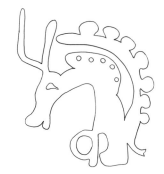

For colour photographs see page 39.
The inspiration for the panel comes from the decoration that appears on the 'fire dog' found at Capel Garmon. The animal head appears to be that of a stag. There is a similar item in the British museum and it is suggested that the purpose of the 'fire dog' was to suspend a carcass on a spit over an open fire.

This heavily embroidered panel uses a limited colour scheme to create two embroidered fabrics. The one for the motif is made from fire colours – the background only shades of black. It is worked by machine and I have used the automatic patterns available on my sewing machine as well as textured fabric and threads.

SIZE
The textile panel measures 20 inches (51 cm) wide by 24 inches (61 cm) high. This size can be changed by increasing or decreasing the scale of the motif.

CREATE THE BACKGROUND FABRIC.
1. Choose a variety of black and almost black fabrics offering different textures and patterns. Use what you can find in your stash. I used 25 inch (63cm) long strips, in different widths, of :-

Plain matt cotton
Knitted velvet
Flowery dress lace over very dark grey velvet
Flock printed net with spider's web design over dark grey poplin
Wide satin ribbon
Satin
There are also mixed strips, pieced before use from :-
Dress velvet
Crushed velvet
Reverse of cotton sateen
Heavy net with a geometric pattern over plain black cotton

2. Cut a piece of firm interfacing measuring 21 inches (54cm) by 25 inches (64cm) for a backing.

Cut the fabric for the strips into lengths of 25 inches (63cm) but varied widths and stitch each to the backing, using the stitch and flip method, as shown in the diagram below. Take care that the fabrics do not 'ride up' – slippery fabrics and velvet can be hard to manage. It helps to use tacking stitches and a walking foot. Press the work as you go, but take care to avoid spoiling the surfaces by flattening the velvet or shrivelling the 'man mades'. Continue in this way until your interfacing fabric is covered with black strips.

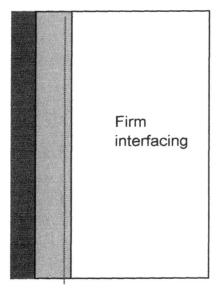

Stage 1

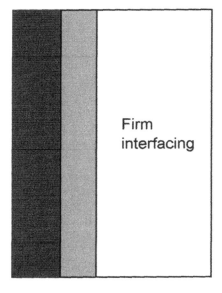

Stage 2

Diagrams to show how the background strips are stitched and turned over ready for the next one to be stitched on.

3. Stitch into this background in a variety of ways, sometimes emphasising the patterns in the fabric, sometimes just stitching straight lines. I used the following machine techniques :-
    Automatic stitches
    'Cable' with straight stitching
    Free machining.
    This will create a firm fabric. Press it on the reverse and ensure that it is flat

CREATE THE FABRIC FOR THE MOTIF
Decide on a colour scheme. I looked for the colours you find in the fire – mainly orange and yellow but some touches of other colours that occurred in the space – dyed fabrics – also gold. Choose a variety of fabrics offering different textures and patterns. Use what you can find in your stash. This time I used smaller and sometimes irregular scraps. I included:
    Plain and patterned velvet
    Space dyed scrim
    Satin
    Linen
    Polycotton

Gold mesh
Ribbon
Silk
Sheers
Lamé

I tacked all these, in a random way to a piece of orange cotton fabric measuring 25 inches (63.5 cm) by 12 inches (30.48 cm). I did not use the stitch and flip method used for the background. The raw edges can be allowed to show, but are often overlapped by other scraps and sometimes secured with stitching.

Stitch all over the motif fabric using straight and automatic stitches in a variety of threads. This gives a firm piece of motif fabric to apply to the background.

APPLY THE MOTIF
Make a paper tracing of the motif . Check that the head is facing the opposite way to how you want it to appear in the finished work.

Layer the paper tracing, the background fabric and the motif fabric together as shown in the diagram, with the traced line showing.

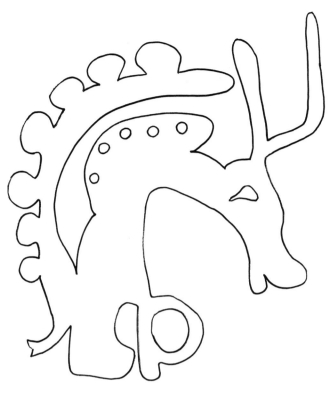

This drawing is one third of the size it needs to be for the panel

To do this, first place your motif fabric, right side up, centrally on top of the background fabric – also right side up – and pin the corners through both layers. Turn over the work and pin the motif tracing centrally between the pins. Check that the extremities of the design do not protrude beyond the motif fabric. Tack the three layers together.

Stitch through the layers from the reverse of the work with a small machine stitch. Use an orange coloured machine thread to stitch through the paper and the two fabrics around the outline of the motif – do not stitch in the eye or the five small circles.

Turn the work over and cut around the outside of the motif, close up to the stitching. Working from the right side stitch around the cut edge, using a zig zag stitch. This does not need to be as close as satin stitch. Tear the paper away from the reverse of the work – it

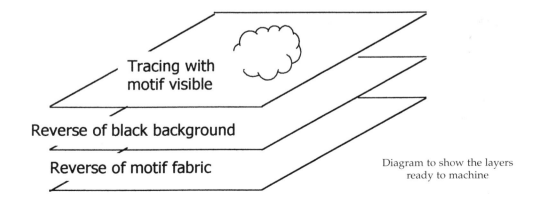

Tracing with motif visible

Reverse of black background

Reverse of motif fabric

Diagram to show the layers ready to machine

will have been perforated by the stitching.

DECORATE THE MOTIF
Use a good variety of decorative stitching to further embellish the motif – sometimes to cover a raw edge which offends you, sometimes to emphasise a line, sometimes to disguise lines where the fabrics join and some to blend the whole piece together. Stitch on some beads or other additional decoration if you wish. Finally embroider the eye and the five circles.

Stretch the work ready to be framed.

liNdisfaRNe coRNers quilt

For colour photographs see page 40.

The ' Lindisfarne Gospels ' is a treasure that can be seen at the British Library in London. It is the work of just one monk and it was created as an act of worship before 721 AD The illustrations are fascinating and are said to use sources from all the then known world.

There are a number of pages with no text – just filled with design. These are referred to as 'carpet pages'. I liked the corners used on one of the pages and thought that they would form the basis of a patchwork design. As they made a good border I then had to find something for them to surround and I chose a Celtic knot that fills a square.

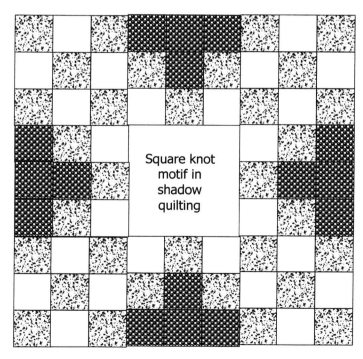

Square knot motif in shadow quilting

Diagram 1 showing the layout for the eight nine patch blocks around the central block

The choice of fabric is yours and if you want the quilt for a bed you will want to choose something washable and serviceable. Mine is a large wall hanging and so I could be more adventurous and chose to cut the majority of my squares from velvet that I had space dyed

The grid for the quilt is shown here. My quilt measures 45 inches (115 cm) square but the size of the small square unit can be adapted to change the size of the finished quilt. My small squares measure 5 inches (12.5cm). Alternatively or in addition a grid using more squares, following the overall colour design would also work well and increase the size of the quilt.

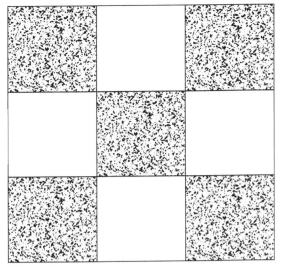

Diagram 2
Block A

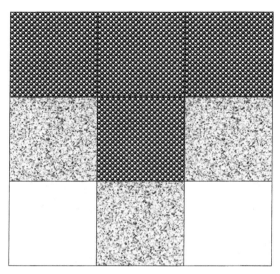

Diagram 2
Block B

MATERIALS NEEDED

1.5 m of 60 inch (150cm) wide space dyed velvet

1.5 m of 60 inch (150cm) wide fleece

0.5 m of 60 inch (150cm) wide sheer fabric

0.75 m of 45 inch (115cm) wide cotton fabric for B blocks and central block

16 inch (41cm) square of fabric for motif for central block

50 inch (127cm) square of wadding

2 m of 54" (140cm) wide lining

21 m of braid

PREPARE FABRIC FOR THE QUILTED T SHAPES

Cut 16 squares, each measuring 5.5 inches (14cm) from:

Fleece for the base layer

Cotton

Sheer fabric for the top layer.

Make 16 stacks of these three fabrics and tack them together before stitching them together around the edges.

NB the quilting on the T shapes is done when the 9 patch blocks have been made

PREPARE THE QUILTED VELVET

Enlarge some of the designs given in this book that will give you a variety of lines to

quilt on.

You need to work on pieces of velvet that you can manipulate easily in the machine say 18 inches (45cm) square. You will need 7 pieces of this size. Cut pieces of fleece to lie under the velvet and tack the fleece to the velvet. Spread out the fabric, velvet side down and cover the fleece with the prepared paper designs. Pin these in place. Thread the machine with a machine thread that blends with the colour scheme of your velvet. Use the same thread top and bottom. Work with the normal machine stitch to stitch through the two layers, following the lines of the design and turning the work under the needle. (I do not recommend freehand machine quilting unless you are comfortable with this style of work.)

When all the fabric is quilted cut 56 squares from it, each measuring 5.5 inches (14cm). And divide them into two groups for example, darker and lighter or according to colour. The effect of the corners depends on the arrangement of colours.

Arrange them according to diagram 1. You may need to spend some time on this process in order to gain the best effect. Put in place the squares prepared for the T shapes. Leave them set out like this until you have

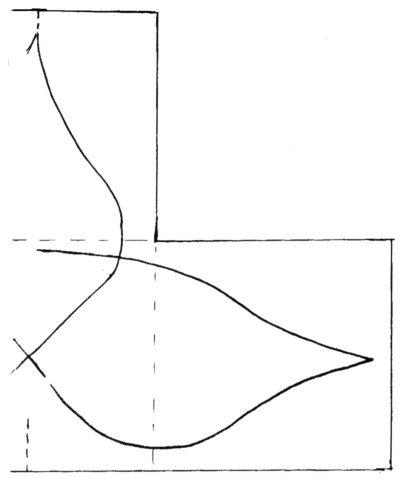

Diagram 3 – design for quilting the T shapes

been able to sew them together.

MAKE THE 'NINE PATCH' BLOCKS

Make up the four A blocks, using all velvet, and the four B blocks, mixing the velvet with the sheer over cotton blocks as shown in diagram 2, using quarter inch (0.64cm) seams.

Tack the pieces together before you stitch them. You may prefer to stitch the velvet pieces together by hand because of the tendency velvet has to move along under the presser foot of the machine. I used an even-feed foot on my machine to counter this. Press the seams using a damp cloth – take care not to melt any of the man made fabrics.

Use the design given in diagram 3 increased to 200% – or something similar to quilt each of the T shapes. After outlining the shape I stitched many rows of echo quilting inside the overall triangular shape and filled the outer area with vermicelli quilting.

MAKE THE CENTRAL BLOCK

The central block is a piece of shadow quilting. To prepare this, trace the motif given in diagram 4 and repeat it so that it makes the square knot. Cut the knot shape from some firm fabric and position it centrally on a piece of cotton, supported by a piece of fleece. Keeping the knot shape, cover it with a piece of sheer fabric and tack

Diagram 4
one quarter
of the square knot

carefully to ensure that the shape of the knot is maintained when you machine through all the layers around the lines of the knot. Check that the overall size of this central block is the same as blocks A and B that are made of nine squares.

JOIN THE NINE BLOCKS
Arrange the blocks to ensure that the pattern is clear and machine them together. Join groups of 3 in 3 rows and then stitch the 3 rows together.

STITCH ON THE BRAID
I covered all of the seams except those inside the T shapes with a purchased braid in order to emphasise the cross shape.

MAKING UP THE QUILT
The top is now complete so make the normal quilt sandwich – lining / wadding / quilt top, squaring up the work. Use lots of safety pins to hold it all together. As there is already a great deal of quilting I recommend holding the layers together with 'ties' at the intersections of the 5 inch (12.5cm) blocks with some extra ties at the intersections of the square knot.

TO TIE THE QUILT
Use a strong thread in a colour of your choice and a large crewel needle or a small chenille needle. You will probably find that you need a thimble and maybe even pliers to pull the needle through. I do not use a frame but you may like to use a quilting hoop. Having

prepared the layers as for quilting the stitch to use is stab stitch, taking the needle through all the layers to make a number of stitches, first up from below and then down again. Think of it as being like stitching on a button. You can make the stitches that show on the quilt top form a cross, two parallel lines or a hollow square or just a fat short line. I like to leave the ends on the reverse long enough to tie off to form a small tassel feature.

NEATEN THE EDGES

To finish the edges turn in a quarter inch (0.64cm) of the velvet and tack around the outside edge of the quilt top. Trim back the lining to leave a half inch (1.27cm) beyond the velvet and fold in this half inch (1.27cm)turning to the inside of the quilt. Oversew around the edge of the entire quilt and cover the stitches with more of the braid.

MAKE A SLEEVE AND A LABEL

Stitch onto the reverse a 4 inch (10cm) sleeve made from the spare lining fabric and add a label giving the name of the quilt, your own name and the date

ott embroidery using celtic imagery

For colour photographs see page 40.
This style of embroidery produces a very rich, but thick fabric by superimposing layer upon layer of fabric, thread and stitching.

As you work at it, you will develop your own preferences. The stages given here also serve as an introduction to or reminder about machine embroidery and the possibilities of combining hand embroidery with it. Because it does not matter if things go a little bit wrong along the way, the worker develops confidence in their own skills. The end product is a heavily worked piece of fabric that can be used in various ways such as for the wall hanging, 'Celtic Fragments' or the Velvet Cushion described later in the book.

DECIDE ON A COLOUR SCHEME:-

You will need a good selection of fabrics, threads and odds and ends such as braid, cord, lace, net, in a colour scheme of your choice. It is a good idea to find a piece of printed fabric that you like and seek out all the colours in it. Make a selection of your colours and stick samples of fabric and threads together onto a page of your notebook. This will enable you to add to your stock, as you progress, without spoiling your colour scheme.

CHOOSE SOME DESIGNS TO START WITH:-

There are many line drawings in this book that you can use but you may prefer to find your own from the source books listed in the bibliography. Remember that the designs are only starting points and you will hope to lose the overall recognition. You can change the scale of motifs and borders and use several sizes within the same piece of work.

CHOOSE A PIECE OF FABRIC FOR THE BACKGROUND :–

You need a piece approximately 11″ x 14″ – a fairly firm fabric, such as a furnishing fabric. If you think yours is too pliable you can support it by a layer of iron on interfacing on the reverse. It is not really feasible to use a frame for this work because of the size and the thickness, especially as it builds up.

MAKE A 'PRACTICE PIECE' :-

Prepare a smaller piece of the fabric you have chosen – to practise on. Use it each time you are going to do something new. Sometimes the thread you have chosen may keep breaking – try reducing the tension and if this does not work, choose another thread. When all else fails, I put the special thread on the bobbin and with standard thread through the needle, I stitch from the reverse. Sometimes fancy stitches are affected by the thickness of your work – it is best to check.

MAKE A PIECE OF OTT EMBROIDERY

APPLIQUÉ USING FUSIBLE WEB SUCH AS 'BONDAWEB'

Choose an appliqué design that fills the space well. Cut a piece of the fusible web large enough to cover your motif. Trace your design onto the paper side of the fusible web. You need to trace a mirror image if your design is not reversible but most of the designs given in this book can be used either way round. Mark the straight of the grain onto the tracing. Test the heat of the iron on some scraps of the fabrics you are using and have the iron as hot as possible. Before you cut around the shape, iron the tracing onto the reverse of the fabric you wish to use, being aware of the grain line. Now cut out the motif along the traced lines. Carefully peel off the paper backing and use your original design to help you arrange the appliqué shape onto the background fabric – thin strips of the motif – such as the legs of an animal are easy to misplace! Now bond the shapes to the background fabric, remembering the iron heat setting you chose when you tested earlier.

Stitch around the edges to secure them. You can use either a fairly close zigzag or one of the fancy stitches on your machine. If your machine will only do a straight stitch, stitch around each shape twice. You can use a contrast thread from within your colour scheme if you wish.

COUCHING

Enhance the appliqué shape by outlining it half an inch (1.5cm) away from the edge with a couched thread. Couching means using sewing cotton to stitch down a thicker thread. If done by hand the couching stitches are worked at right angles to the couched thread. To couch by machine you can use a zigzag stitch or an open fancy stitch from your machine's vocabulary.

MORE SHAPES

Make one or two more appliqué designs in the same way – perhaps smaller – superimposed on the first. Make an outline for them too. You may prefer to use hand embroidery to do this or you can use a machine cable stitch (sometimes called bobbin work). For this, you wind a thicker thread, or one of variable thickness onto the bobbin (underneath). You will then need to loosen the bobbin tension. Machines vary but there is usually a way to do this – check in your machine manual – it will be in the section that tells you how to check your tension for a good stitch formation. If you have to turn a screw, note how may degrees you turn it so that you can return to normal tension afterwards. This technique requires that you work from the reverse of the piece but you can tell where you want to stitch because the outline of the motif you are embellishing shows though. Allow the designs to overlap and do not worry if the bits you like are covered by the new layers you work.

LINE DRAWING WITH STITCH.

Use yet another design to work just the outline of a design in cable stitch or hand embroider an outline in bold thread.

FILL IN SOME GAPS

Take a good look at what you have done and fill in some gaps. From the collection of fabrics and threads in your colour scheme, choose one of the following:-

Some fibres unravelled from one of your fabrics or a small bundle of yarns, or a scrap of net, scrim, sheer fabric or lace, or a mixture of any of these.

Cut a rough shape of a fabric or make an irregular group measuring about 2 inches (5cm) across and tack it in place – partly in a gap and partly overlapping a motif – before stitching it down by machine in a contrasting thread. To do this you can free machine with filigree or long zigzags or work a small Celtic motif.

SLIPS

Make some 'slips' and apply them. Slips are small pieces of embroidery that are worked separately – perhaps a square knot, a letter shape or a Celtic cross This can be any style of embroidery- hand or machine – maybe even part of your practice piece. Cut around the motif and position it as you did the small pieces in stage five. Tack it in place, then machine stitch over it to hold it in place – not necessarily around the edge.

UNIFYING

Finally cover the entire work with machining to unify the piece. This could be a grid of zigzags or a fancy automatic stitch on your machine. Alternatively, you could place a tracing of a complicated knot design on the reverse of the work and use a slightly thicker thread on the bobbin while you stitch through the paper and the embroidery from the reverse, allowing your bobbin thread to make the design.

PRESS THE WORK

Place a towel on your ironing board. Lay the work on top of it – reverse side up – and press to flatten it after all that stitching,

triangular knot cushion in machined reverse applique

For colour photographs see page 40.
This cushion uses the embroidered fabric I call OTT and has an 'Oxford edge' to finish the outer edge. It is fastened with buttons on the reverse side. The overall measurement is 20 inches (50cm) square.

MATERIALS NEEDED

Furnishing velvet measuring 21 inches (53cm) square.

Motif fabric measuring 13 inches (33cm) square – I used OTT fabric as described in an earlier chapter but a firm patterned furnishing fabric would work.

Machine thread to match the velvet.

Decorative yarns to embellish the outline of the motif in colours to echo the pattern colours.

Two pieces of plain furnishing fabric for the reverse of the cushion in colour to tone with velvet, each measuring 21 inches (53cm) by 13 inches (33cm).

Four buttons measuring about three quarters of an inch (2cm).

A 16 inch (40cm) square cushion pad.

PREPARE THE DESIGN

Enlarge the design shown here so that it measures 12 inches (30cm) at its widest part.

Make a copy of the design on tracing paper – use a black indelible marker that gives a strong line.

PREPARE TO STITCH

Make a stack on the table – first, the velvet, right side down, next motif fabric, right side down, in the centre of the velvet and then the tracing, drawing side up. Pin all the layers together, using safety pins. Choose a machine thread that matches the velvet for both reel and bobbin and set the machine to a small

straight stitch. (Do not attempt to free machine.) I avoid using a hoop for several reasons: –

it crushes the pile of the velvet,

the motif is too big

the OTT fabric and paper together are firm enough to avoid puckering the work.

STITCH THE OUTLINE
From the paper side of the work, stitch over all the lines that define the edge of the three portions of the triangular knot.

CUT BACK
Tear away the tracing and using sharp scissors, cut away the surplus motif fabric from the reverse, leaving an overlap of about half an inch (1.5cm). Turn the work to the right side and, very carefully, cut within the motif to remove the velvet thus exposing the motif fabric, clipping close to the sewn line.

SECURE THE RAW EDGE
Cover the raw edges of the velvet surrounding the motif by machining, either:- with a close zigzag or with several rows of straight stitching or by using one of the automatic stitches from your machine.

EMBELLISH THE MOTIF EDGE
I used a variegated knitting yarn to pick up the colours in the embroidery. You can do this by hand or machine. Couch stitch a yarn over your stitching around the edge of the three parts of the motif. Couch another line about half an inch (1.5cm) outside the outer edge of the whole motif to make one large triangle.

MAKE THE REVERSE SIDE OF THE CUSHION
Lay out the two pieces of fabric intended for the reverse of the cushion, side by side. Check that the grain of the farbic lies the same way on both pieces. Mark the two edges that are in the centre. Stitch a small single turning down this side of each piece of fabric. Fold this stitched edge over onto the reverse of the fabric for 2 inches (5cm). Tack this turning in place. Work four buttonholes onto one of the pieces and stitch the buttons on to the other, ensuring that the reverse of the cushion measures 21 inches (53cm) square. See the diagram for the buttonhole placement. Fasten the buttons.

STITCH THE FRONT AND REVERSE TOGETHER
Place right sides together and tack carefully. Machine around all four edges taking a half inch (1.5cm) turning. Use the evenfeed foot if your machine has one. Trim the surplus fabric from the turnings at the corners to allow for good corners when the cushion is turned right way out. Open the buttons and turn the cushion right way out and finger-press so as to make a clear edge. Tack the front and reverse layers together two inches (5cm) from the edges, thus enclosing the raw edges of the seams.

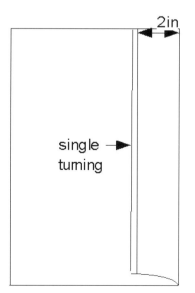
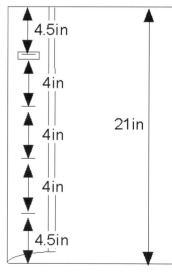

Diagram 1 showing hems and butttonholes

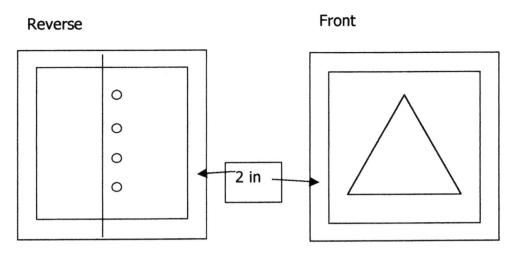

Reverse   **Front**

2 in

Diagram 2 Oxford Edge

FINISH THE CUSHION WITH AN OXFORD EDGE

Machine stitch around the cover, through the two layers, over your tacking to make the edge you often find on pillowcases. See diagram 2. Remove all tacking stitches and insert the cushion pad.

celtic fragments wall hanging

For colour photographs see page 40.
I have described how to create the OTT fabric needed for this hanging earlier. The fabric that is produced in this way is very firm indeed so seams need special treatment.

MAKING THE CRAZY PATCHWORK STRIPS

I cut strips of several pieces of OTT all measuring 5 inches (12.7cm) in width. I then cut the strips into a variety of geometric shapes – all using an angle of 60/30 degrees. The lengths of the sides varied and the new cuts were made sometimes with the high point on the left and sometimes with it on the right. (diagram 1). I was then able to make up some 5 inch (12.7cm) wide strips of crazy patchwork by fitting the pieces together. The style of the new fabric prohibits ordinary seams so the edges were butted up together and then stitched over with a zig zag stitch. Fancy threads were then couched in place to cover the joint and add interest.

MAKING THE JOINING STRIPS

For the joining strips I chose some fabric in a colour that would unite them – turquoise – with a selection of threads in close variations of turquoise. I worked some two inch (5cm) wide strips of interesting – though less elaborate and more formal embroidery along the length. The new strips needed to be firm because they would need to be joined to the OTT fabric by the method described above. I needed about 170 inches (4.4m) in all. To make the wide cross bars I cut five inch (12.7cm) lengths and joined them in pairs. Then I cut across the OTT patchwork strips at right angles and used some of the turquoise strips to join them back together again.

MAKING THE DESIGN

I then cut three strips of the new mixed OTT and embroidery to a length of 30 inches (76.2cm) and four strips of the turquoise embroidery and joined all together, using the method described above. See diagram 2. I inserted into the seams some folded triangles of embroidery

Diagram 1 showing cutting lines for OTT fabric

MAKING UP THE HANGING

To complete the piece I hand stitched on a backing having first layered a piece of lightweight wadding between the two but without quilting. I was fortunate to find a piece of carving that was the right size for the work to make a suitable form of hanging rail but otherwise, I would have stitched a sleeve to the top to take a rod.

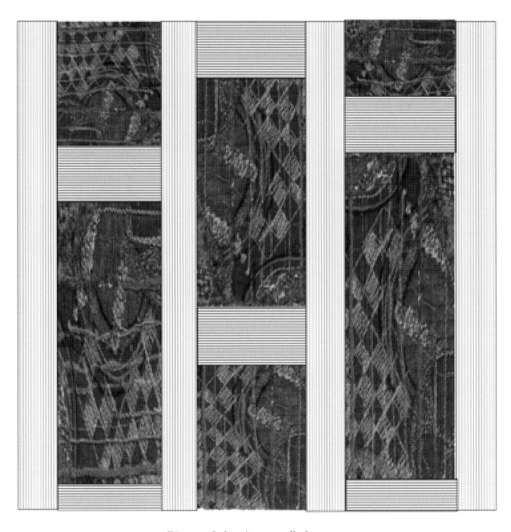

Diagram 2 showing overall plan.

quoniam wall hanging

For colour photographs see page 40.
This quilt uses strongly patterned modern fabrics from across the world to reproduce an ancient representation of a capital letter.. The inspiration for this quilt is an initial letter from the Book of Kells – Q for Quoniam.

My quilt is worked by machine but the whole quilt could be worked by hand. The techniques used are basic piecing but this is not a project for beginners. Whichever you choose, you will need to work accurately. The curved additions are 'faced' with the same black cotton that is used for the reverse of the quilt.

My quilt measures 30 inches (76cm) across including the protrusions. I chose an African print for the wide strips that make up most of the piece. I used a different part of the same fabric for the curved sections and the background on the focal block. The narrow strips are of plain fabric and the background a vague print that reads as plain. The diamond for the focal square is a piece if Asian Fabric.

The 'background' is quilted with a Celtic style motif to fit the shape. There is a good deal of free machine quilting, sometimes following the printed pattern of the fabric, sometimes the lines of the narrow strips that border various areas.

Diagram 1 overall plan

MATERIALS NEEDED

1 metre strongly patterned fabric for the main strips

0.5m plain fabric for the narrow strips and cross centres

0.5m subtly pattered contrasting fabric for the background

0.25 metre strongly patterned fabric for the curved sections and the triangles in the focal block

small piece of special fabric for the focal block

small piece of calico for the foundation of the focal block

1 metre of lining fabric

1 metre 2 oz wadding

Strip of firm but flexible plastic 30 inches (76cm) by 6 inches (15cm).

FOCAL DIAMOND BLOCK (A ON DIAGRAM 1)

Mark up the foundation as follows:-
Draw a rectangle 6 inches (15cm) by 9.5 inches (24cm) on a piece of calico. See diagram 2. Measure from the bottom left hand side along the bottom line towards the centre and mark the point 2.5 inches (6.3cm) from the left hand side. Repeat this measuring from the right along the bottom and from right and left along the top line. Mark the points 3.5 inches (8.9cm) from the corners down both sides and up from the bottom on each side. Join the points together to make the corner triangles. Draw lines parallel to these towards the centre, 0.75 inch (2cm) away from the first corner lines. Draw a one inch (2.5cm) border outside the first rectangle.

The method is foundation piecing. The calico you have drawn on is the foundation. The patchwork fabric is stitched to the side that you have not drawn on – the stitching is worked from the reverse of the work – using the drawn lines to stitch along.

Diagram 2 drawing the foundation for focal block

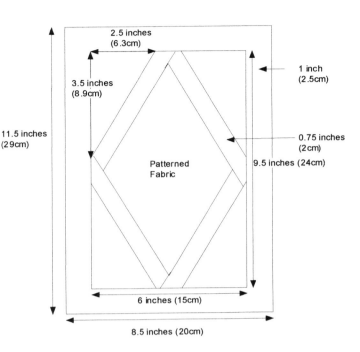

2.5 inches (6.3cm)

3.5 inches (8.9cm)

11.5 inches (29cm)

1 inch (2.5cm)

0.75 inches (2cm)

Patterned Fabric

9.5 inches (24cm)

6 inches (15cm)

8.5 inches (20cm)

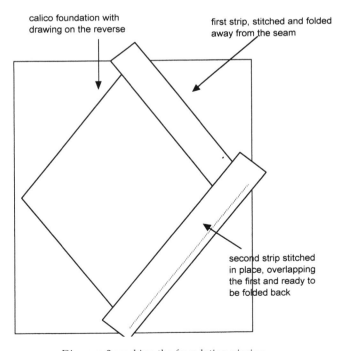

calico foundation with drawing on the reverse

first strip, stitched and folded away from the seam

second strip stitched in place, overlapping the first and ready to be folded back

Diagram 3 working the foundation piecing

73

WORK THE FOCAL BLOCK:-

Start in the centre placing a diamond shaped piece of fabric centrally. The fabric needs to be a little larger than the diamond. Be generous – you can trim back the surplus as you go along. Tack it in place.

Cut contrast strips 1.5 inches (4cm) wide and stitch each in turn to the diamond, through the calico. See diagram 3. Cut back the surplus fabric from the first diamond. Fold each piece over and press as you go.

Cut rectangles of the fabric chosen for the corners, measuring 5.5 inches (14cm) by 3 inches (7.5cm) and add these in the same way. Cut back the surplus fabric from the first diamond border. Fold each piece over and press

For the outer border of this block cut strips measuring 1.75 inches (4.5cm) and stitch them on as before. Cut back the surplus fabric from the rectangles. Fold each piece over and press. Tack around the outside.

The focal block is now complete. Leave it for the time being.

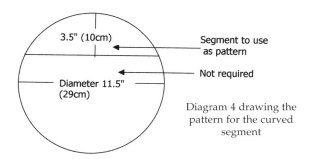

Diagram 4 drawing the pattern for the curved segment

THE CIRCLE AND CURVED INSERTS (F ON DIAGRAM 1)

MAKE A PATTERN FOR THE CURVED INSERTS

Draw a circle on pattern paper measuring 11.5 inches (29cm) in diameter. Measure 3.5 inches (10cm) in from the edge and draw a straight line to make a segment of the circle. See diagram 4.

Cut out the paper and use it as a pattern to cut four pieces of the chosen fabric and four of lining fabric, adding your quarter inch turnings or the alternative metric measurement for your turnings.

Place each pair of fabric pieces right sides together and stitch around the curved edges, allowing a quarter inch turning. Press the line of stitches and turn the work through. Press again on the right side to ensure that there is a smooth curve. Tack along the straight edges to hold them together, a quarter of an inch from the edge. These quarter inch turnings will be inserted into seams at a later stage.

FOR THE CIRCLE AT THE BOTTOM

Draw a circle on pattern paper measuring 8 inches (20cm) in diameter.

Cut out the paper and use it as a pattern to cut a piece of the chosen fabric and one of lining fabric, adding your quarter inch turnings. Make a cut in the centre of the lining fabric measuring about 3 inches (7.5cm).

Place the circles right sides together and stitch around the edges, allowing a quarter inch turning. Press the line of stitches and turn the work through via the slit in the lining fabric. Carefully smooth out any tucks around the edge and press, ensuring that no lining fabric can be seen from the right side. Catch stitch the edges of the slit together without distorting the shape of the circle.

Leave the pieces for the time being.

THE TWO PATCHWORK CROSSES

Cut 8 strips of your two chosen fabrics, each measuring 1.5 inches (4cm) x 12 inches (30.5cm) – (16 strips in all). Join them together into pairs along the long edges with a quarter inch seam. Press along the stitching, then open the seam and press again.

Make the three templates as shown in diagram 5 – (the two parallelograms are the same as each other, but one is flipped).

Arrange the templates on a pieced strip and cut out 8 of each shape, adding quarter inch turnings around each shape.

To stitch the crosses, follow the piecing diagram – 8

Leave them for the time being.

Make two crosses and leave them for the time being.

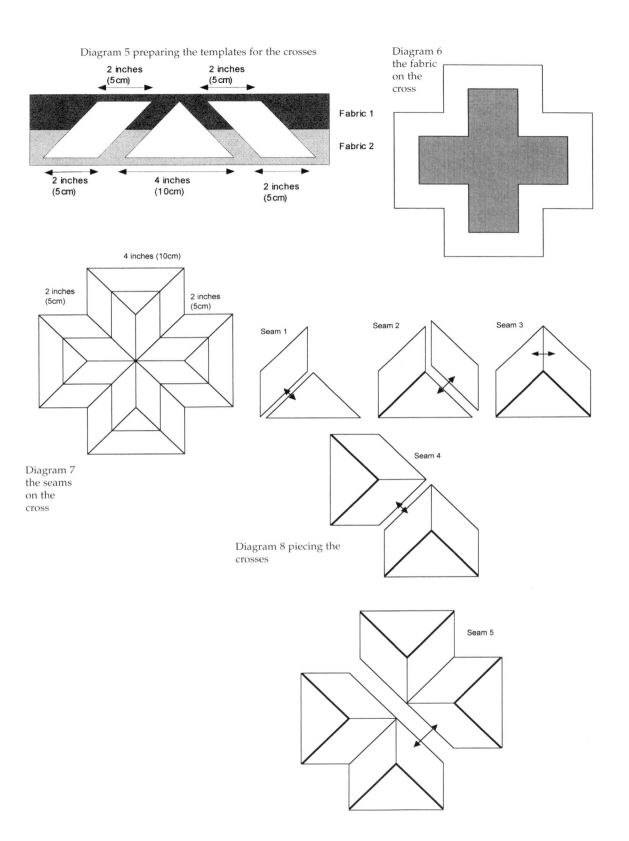

Diagram 5 preparing the templates for the crosses

2 inches
(5cm)

2 inches
(5cm)

Fabric 1

Fabric 2

2 inches
(5cm)

4 inches
(10cm)

2 inches
(5cm)

Diagram 6
the fabric
on the
cross

4 inches (10cm)

2 inches
(5cm)

2 inches
(5cm)

Seam 1

Seam 2

Seam 3

Diagram 7
the seams
on the
cross

Seam 4

Diagram 8 piecing the
crosses

Seam 5

BUILDING THE QUILT – refer to diagram 1
Cut some strips of the main print fabric, 4.5 inches (11.5cm) wide.

Use a piece of the strip cut 11.5 inches (29cm) long (B) to add to the right hand side of the focal block- right sides together, quarter inch seam. Press the strip and the seam away from the focal block.

Cut two strips 12.5 inches (32cm) long and stitch one (C) to the bottom of the focal block (D) and the bottom end of the first strip, and one to the top, pressing outwards as before.

The strip for the left hand side (E) extends to the bottom of the quilt. Cut it 35.5 inches (90cm) long and stitch it to the focal block, starting at the top. Leave the bottom end loose.

Cut a strip (L) to join the crosses measuring 23.5 inches (60cm) and stitch a cross to each end of it

Now stitch on the curved segments (F). Place each one in the centre of each of the strips surrounding the focal blocks. Put right sides together with the edges lined up. Stitch, taking a quarter inch turning. Do not press them outwards yet.

From the background fabric cut a piece according to the measurements given in diagram 9 for the shape marked (J) and a piece measuring 3.5 inches (10cm) x 16 inches (41cm) for (G). Stitch (G) to a 16 inch (41cm) length of the 4.5 inch (11.5cm) wide strip (H) and stitch the right hand side of (H) to the left hand side of (J). Join the bottom of (H) to the left hand side of the bottom cross with a strip of 4.5 inches (11.5cm) wide fabric measuring 10 inches (25.5cm)(L)

Cut some 2 inch (5cm) strips of fabric for the narrow border that surrounds the majority of the sections. Stitch appropriately cut lengths of this strip as follows:–

From top to bottom of (E), enclosing the raw edges of one of the segments.

From top to bottom of (B) , enclosing the raw edges of another of the segments.

Along the top of (E), and (D) enclosing the raw edges of another of the segments.

From top to bottom of the right hand side of (H)

Along the bottom of part of (C) – 2.5 inches (6.5cm)

Down both sides of (L) extending into the crosses at each end

From the top of (H) to the point where H meets the bottom 4.5 inch (11.5cm) strip (L)

Along the bottom of (J)

Now stitch in the background section (J) to fill the space remaining. Note that although the top of the right hand side lines up with the side of the top cross, the top of the left hand side of J falls short of the strip at the top of (B).

The top of the quilt is now complete, except for the addition of the circle. Wait until after the quilting has been completed to stitch this on.

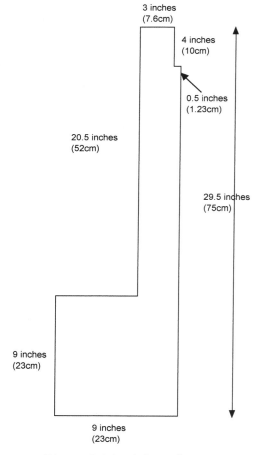

3 inches
(7.6cm)

4 inches
(10cm)

0.5 inches
(1.23cm)

20.5 inches
(52cm)

29.5 inches
(75cm)

9 inches
(23cm)

9 inches
(23cm)

Diagram 9 size and shape of background

MAKING UP THE QUILT

I felt that the irregular edge of the quilt needed a different treatment from the usual quilt sandwich and chose to stitch on the lining before working the quilting.

Tack the curved sections in towards the middle of the quilt – out of the way of the edges.

Spread out the wadding on a flat surface and and cover it with the lining, right side showing.

Smooth out the quilt top on the lining, right side down.

Tack all together, taking care that the grain is straight and the curved pieces are not caught in by mistake.

Stitch around the edges taking particular care at the corners where the crosses protrude. Leave an opening at the bottom where the circle will be placed. Reinforce the concave corners (on the crosses) with extra stitching and cut into the turning diagonally to enable the fabric to lie flat when turned through.

Trim back any surplus and turn the work through. Pay special attention to the sharp corners. Stitch up the opening by hand. Remove any tacking and press the edges of the work. Place on a flat surface and smooth out the work. Tack the layers together ready for the quilting.

Tack securely around the edges to ensure that the seam is on the very edge – no lining showing from the front, no front showing from the reverse.

QUILTING

Use tailor's chalk to mark the design for the background panel (Diagram 10) and any other guides you feel you may need.

QUILTING BY HAND

Use a quilting hoop and ordinary sewing thread. Cut the thread rather than break it and use a length of 16 to 18 inches (40 to 45 cm). Use a small 'betweens' needle (as small as you can manage to thread!) and a thimble.

Start with the motif you have transferred onto the background. To start, tie a small knot on the end of the thread and bring the

Diagram 10 quilting design for background

needle up though all the layers. Pull the thread though and, with an extra tug, pop the knot through the bottom layer of fabric. Work one small backstitch to secure. To fasten off the thread when it has been almost used up, the process is reversed. Tie a knot close to the work and take a small back stitch, bringing the needle out of the quilt an inch (2.5cm) or so away, popping the knot into the wadding. Pull the thread tight as you cut it close to the fabric and the end will slip back into the work. The stitch is what you may think of as a running stitch. Ideally each stitch passes through the fabric layers at right angles. Experienced hand quilters use a rocking motion to bend the fabric as they go, collecting three or four stitches on the needle before pulling the needle through. It is more important for the stitches to be even than to be small.

Leave the major shape empty of stitching – just an outline – but use stippling for the surrounding area. Stippling consists of working the quilting stitch in an irregular fashion – you may like to think of it as scribbling.

Now move to the 4 inch (14cm) strips. You may find that there are some printed lines that you can follow. If not, you could use the border pattern from 'Blue Lions', in an earlier chapter.

Quilt in the ditch around all the narrow strips and some lines along the centre.

QUILTING BY MACHINE
Prepare your working space. You need to have table space to the left of the sewing machine that will support the work as you go. Thread up the machine with the same machine thread on the top and the bobbin – perhaps a colourless thread because of the many colours in the patchwork. Use an evenfeed foot if you have one. The piece is not really suitable to use a frame so remember to spread out your hands around the area you are working on.

Start by outlining the motif on the background section on which you drew chalk lines. Pull the bobbin thread up onto the surface where you can see it so that you do not stitch over it. Try to avoid breaks in the stitching. Some are inevitable and you need to leave ends of thread long enough to be able to take them through to the back, to tie them off and thread them into the wadding.

Next stitch in the ditch (the line of the seam) around all the narrow borders. Add one or two more lines along the borders that were cut at 2 inches (5cm). The method I used is a favourite of mine. I select the automatic stitch that is intended for stitching elastic. I alter the stitch length and width to the maximum. This gives a wavy line.

Move now to the 4 inch (14cm) strips. Look to see if there are pattern lines that you can follow. If not use one of the borders from elsewhere in the book.

Now set up your machine for free quilting and return to the background shape to fill in the area around the motif with vermicelli quilting. (i.e make a continuous squiggly line that does not cross over itself.) You may like to practise this with pencil and paper to get the hang of it.

When the stitching is complete, thread pairs of ends through a needle with a large eye and take them though to the back. Tie a knot near to the fabric and thread the remainder into the wadding.

THE CIRCLE
Find the circle you prepared earlier and hand stitch it in position as shown in diagram 1, covering the place where you stitched up the opening by hand.

MAKE A SUPPORT FOR THE TOP
The top is not a straight line so it will need support. The way I dealt with this was to make an additional lining for the top few inches (10-15cm) to hold a piece of firm but flexible plastic – similar to template plastic. I made a pattern by drawing along the top edge, taking in the curved section and the top of the cross. I was then able to cut the plastic to size. I used the plastic as a template to cut a piece of lining, allowing quarter inch turnings on all sides. I stitched this pocket for the plastic by hand.

COMPLETE THE WALL HANGING
Stitch a hanging sleeve on the reverse of the additional lining that holds the plastic. The sleeve consists of a strip of lining fabric the full width of the hanging and 4 or 5 inches (10-12cm) deep, through which you can thread a rod to hang the work.

Make a label with the name of the wall hanging, your own name and the year. Stitch this onto the reverse of the quilt.

part 3

design library

Scissor shape

Dublin Griffin

Inter-twined creatures

ChiRo

Cross of Thorns

Use for a corner or several to make a border

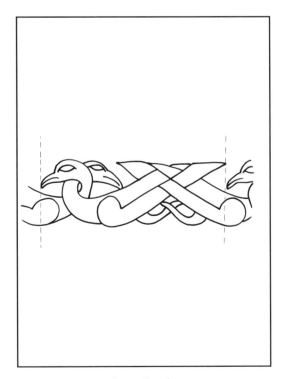

Swan Border

Knotwork Flower

BIBLIOGRAPHY

Brown, P., *The Book of Kells*, Thames and Hudson ISBN 0500-23326-8

Brown, M.P., *Painted Labyrinth*, British Library ISBN 0-7123-4811-5

Davies, Gwyn, *Golau Gwlad*, Cristnogaeth yng Nghymru 200-2000 ISBN 1-85049-180-1

Davis, C., *The Celtic Art Source Book*, Blandford Press ISBN 0-7137-2144-8

Grey, *Celtic Inspiration for Machine Embroidery*, Batsford ISBN 07134-8750-X

James and Rigby, *Britain and the Celtic Iron Age*, British Museum Press
ISBN 0-7141-2306-4

Jones, O., *The Grammar of Ornament Omega*, Books Ltd. ISBN1-85007-072-5

Kightly, C. A., *Mirror of Medieval Wales*, Cadw ISBN 0-048329-30-0

Lawther, G., *Celtic Quilting*, David and Charles ISBN 0-7153-0540-9

Meehan, Aidan, *Celtic Design - A Beginner's Manual*, Thames and Hudson
ISBN 0500-27629-3

Meehan, Aidan, *Celtic Design -The Dragon and the Griffin*, Thames and Hudson
ISBN 0500-27792-3

Mullins, D.J., *Early Welsh Saints*, Gwasg Carreg Gwalch ISBN 0-86381-800 -5

Pitkin Guides, *Celtic Wales*, Pitkin ISBN 0-85372-798-8

Cambell Harding and Smith, Rowena, *Celtic Art*, Brockhampton Press
ISBN 1-86019-483-4

Sloss, A., *How to Draw Celtic Knotwork*, Brockhampton Press ISBN 1-86019-8589

Spinhoven, C., *Celtic Charted Designs*, Dover ISBN 0-486-25411-9

Starmore, A., *Celtic Needlepoint*, Anaya ISBN 1-85470-070-7

Stead and Youngs, *Celts*, British Museum Press ISBN 0-7141-2102-9

Thames and Hudson, *Sacred Symbols – The Celts* ISBN 0-500-06014-2

The story of Mann, *Celts in Mann*, Manx National Heritage ISBN 0-901106-39-9

Wainwright, A., *Celtic Cross Stitch Samplers*, Cassell ISBN 0-304-34443-5

Zaczec, I., *Celtic Art and Design*, Studio Editions ISBN 1-85891-191-5

Magazine, *Cambria* – Midsummer 2000

RESOURCES

I hope that this book has stimulated your interest in the Celts and that you will want to follow this up in other ways. Here are some ideas.

The Internet has some Celtic sources. My design for the Celtic hare came from a free download on
http;/www.aon-celticbin.com/cfreewareclipart/hounds6a.html
They offer a package of design for purchase.

Golden Hinde offers mail order kits for goldwork embroidery including the Celtic cross in the Gallery - Contact them at 9, Hewitt Street, Latchford, Warrington WA4 1BG   Tel 0780 864 8381 / 01925 810697

Celtic Shadow Quilting kits and hard to find fabrics and threads from Barbara Howell, Cae Cam, Ochr y Bryn, Henllan, Denbigh, LL16 5AT 01745 812800

'Celtica' offers you the chance to discover the past, present and future of the Celts at Y Plas, Machynlleth, Powys. www.celtica.wales.com 01654 702702

The House of Manannan in Peel, Isle of Man offers an interesting exhibition with sound and film about the Celts in Man.

The British Museum in London has many Celtic treasures.

The Victoria and Albert Museum in London has life size replicas of Celtic crosses and the Norwegian doorways.

The British Library in London holds the Lindisfarne Gospel and it is open for everyone to see.

Ask at information centres in Wales, Ireland, Scotland and the Isle of Man for directions to places where there are Celtic items to be seen in the locality.

index